To

Bernadette

In memory and appreciation of thirty one fruitful,
eventful and extremely happy years together.

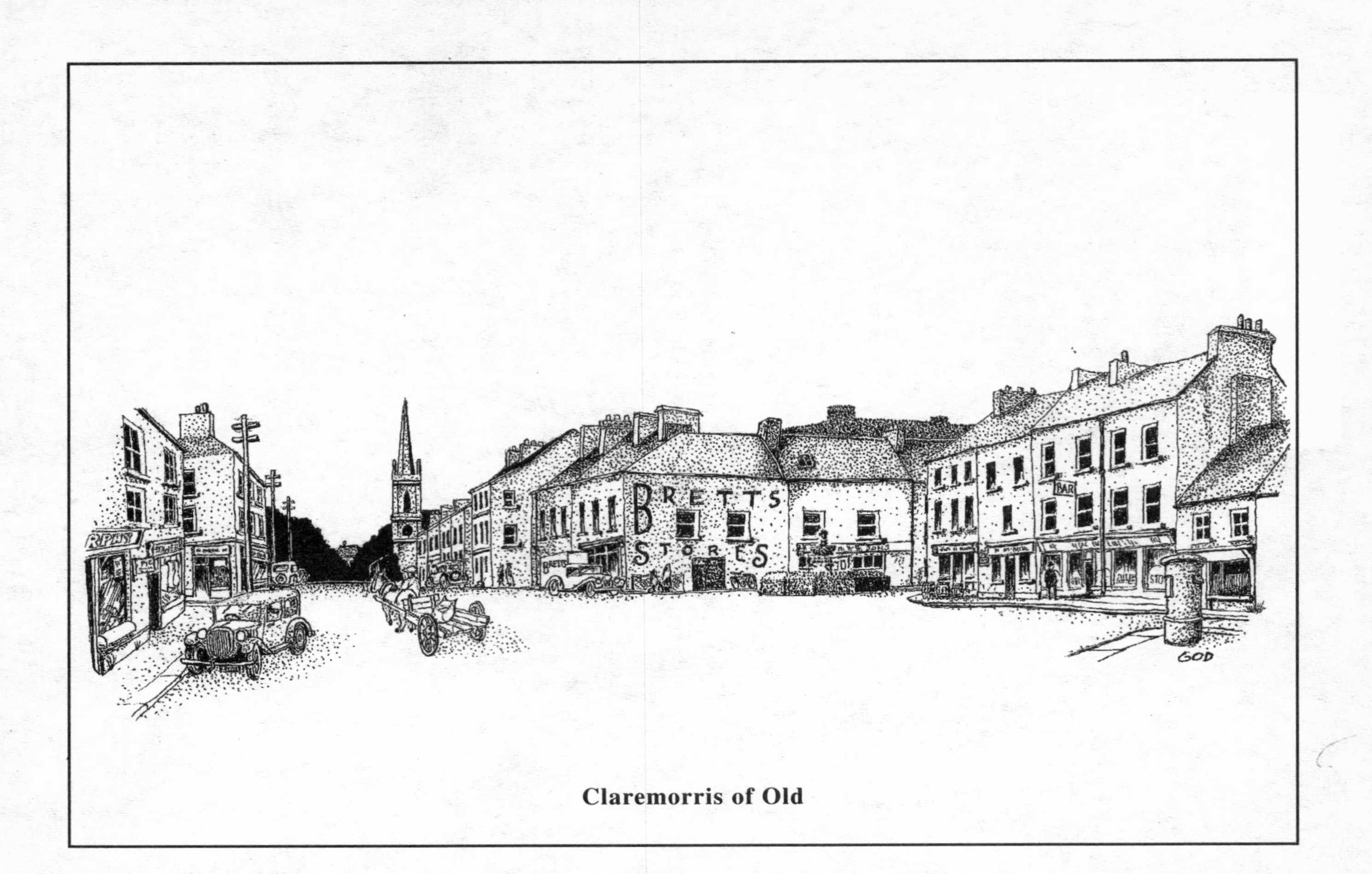

Claremorris of Old

A CONNACHT MAN'S RAMBLE

by
Willie Costello

Recollections of growing up in the rural Ireland of the thirties and forties

With an introduction by Dr. Thomas Mitchell
Provost, Trinity College, Dublin

Illustrated by Gerry O Donovan

Dublin
by Éamonn de Búrca for
EDMUND BURKE PUBLISHER 1997

ISBN : 0 946130 16 7

British Library Cataloguing in Publication Data.
A catalogue record for this book is available
from the British Library

Dublin by Éamonn de Búrca for Edmund Burke Publisher
"Cloonagashel", 27 Priory Drive, Blackrock, Co. Dublin.

Contents

List of Illustrations

Acknowledgments

It is a singular honour to have had a man of the eminence of Doctor Thomas Mitchell, Provost of Trinity College, Dublin read the manuscript and write the introduction to this book and I owe him a deep debt of gratitude.

I also wish to acknowledge the assistance received from the following who helped me in the course of my research and in the writing of this book:

My sincere thanks and appreciation to Bríd Mitchell, An Spidéal, who typed the script and who, without complaint, agreed to every alteration which I requested. I would also like to thank my publisher, Éamonn de Búrca and Vivien, his wife, for their hospitality, professional advice, and overall design, Gerry O Donovan for producing the illustrations, Sonia Schorman for editing and proof- reading, Eddie Chandler for design and typesetting, and James MacIntyre for the front cover watercolour illustration.

I particularly wish to thank my brother John who rendered invaluable assistance with my research and who confirmed many of my recollections of long past local events.

I am deeply indebted to Bernard O'Hara, B. Comm., L.L.B., M.B.A., lecturer, historian, and author of several books, who generously read and corrected the script and made important suggestions which have greatly enhanced my presentation.

Without the guidance and enthusiasm of Máire Holmes, Lecturer, Broadcaster, Author, Playwright and Director of Griffon Creative Writers, this book would not have been written. I thank her for her patience and encouragement.

With gratitude and affection I remember the role of my parents in implanting in me a love for my native locality. Their stories about people and events recalled from their own childhood years have been a source of great inspiration to me. With almost equal gratitude, but understandably with less affection, I recall the pride in our country and in its history instilled into our impressionable minds by James Murphy during our school days. May the soil in the cemeteries of Ballinasmalla and Barnacarroll rest lightly over them. Little did they know that their stories and patriotism were sowing in me the seeds of *A Connacht Man's Ramble.*

I also thank: Canon J. Sweeney, The Presbytery, Claremorris; Hugh Berry and Kevin Cowley, former Inspectors with Irish Land Commission; Dr. Roderick Maguire, Ardeevin, Claremorris; South Mayo Family Research, Main Street, Ballinrobe; Mrs. Margaret Lewis, 35 Colimore Road, Dalkey, Co. Dublin; Tommy Ruane, Main Street, Claremorris; John O'Donnell, Production Manager, Connacht Tribune; Des Mahon, Mayo Co. Manager; John Carty, Knock; Michael Marren, Regional Manager, A.I.B., Galway; John Walkin, Chairman, Ireland West Tourism; J.J. Ronayne, Convent Road, Claremorris; Tony Boyle, 35 Sandyview Drive, Riverside, Galway; Martin Hession, President, St. Colman's College, Claremorris (retired); Eamonn Hughes, James Street, Claremorris; Billy Moran, Western Health Board; Rita Cunningham, Dept. of Adult Education, University College, Galway; All the members of the Griffon Creative Writers Group, Galway; Tom Kelly, Connaught Telegraph; Donal Downes, Managing Director, P.J. Tobin Consulting Engineers; Kit Reaney, Castlegar; Jimmy Cunnane, Caraun, and Sister Ailbe, Mercy Convent, Claremorris.

Finally I wish to thank my own family for their encouragement and support while I was writing this book.

Introduction

This is a frank and varied memoir that presents a vivid and comprehensive portrait of the way of life, the habits, the spiritual and human values and personal interactions of the closely-knit communities of rural Ireland a generation ago. But in this single generation the relatively simple, sometimes harsh, but always vibrant and warm world of Willie Costello has virtually disappeared without trace.

Ireland of the 1930s and '40s was largely a country of small farms, the great bulk of the holdings, especially west of the Shannon, under thirty acres. There was no dole, except in extreme cases, no headage payments or other forms of government largesse. Markets were limited for agricultural products, and prices fluctuated widely. A very narrow industrial base provided little opportunity to supplement the meagre income from the land.

Money was, as a result, exceedingly scarce, and the small farms were compelled to be as self-sufficient as possible, supplying virtually all of their own food, with the exception of tea and sugar, and even some of the clothing from the beautiful, durable thread spun from the wool of their own sheep. The lack of money and the fear and difficulty of borrowing capital virtually precluded mechanisation and any form of modernisation that involved regular charges. Even rural electrification was viewed with mixed feelings, and cars and tractors were a rarity, the low cost, maintenance bicycle providing the main form of transport.

They were conditions of life that were constraining and limiting by modern standards. They bound people to the land in labour intensive, low production mixed farming that supplied basic needs but little more. Above all, they allowed for no growth in employment, and other areas of the economy were similarly stagnant, giving rise to one of the most painful aspects of Irish life of fifty years ago, the early break up of closely-knit families through emigration.

But there was another side to the rural Ireland described by Willie Costello. There were the delights of an unspoiled rural environment and of nature's changing patterns, and for those who loved the land the pleasure of owning and working their own holding, of being their own boss, setting their own schedule, insulated from fears of redundancy and unemployment. There was the support and neighbourliness engendered by the meitheal tradition that regularly brought neighbourhoods together in collective effort for the jobs that no farmer could do on his own.

And there was a richly textured social life centred around the church, the school, sport, the pub, the visiting houses, the dance halls, and the weddings and funerals.

All of this is recounted by Willie Costello in a story that provides first-hand testimony and is plainly told with a deeply personal touch, and without the superstructure of schematic analysis or social theorising so tempting for professional historians. Soon there will be few who have the first-hand memories that can preserve the authentic flavour of this distinctive but disappearing culture. Books like this are therefore important. This one is also most enjoyable reading.

Thomas N. Mitchell,

Provost, Trinity College, Dublin.

Preface

Mine is not a ramble in the physical sense but a leisurely mental stroll back to the days of my childhood and adolescence in a remote townland in the West of Ireland. As I never kept a personal diary it was necessary for me to recall entirely from memory the stories about people, customs and events spanning more than half a century. Individuals who figure in this narrative actually existed and were known to me personally with the exception of the few who had passed on before my time. The names are genuine but in a few rare instances, as in the accounts of matchmaking, and the ghostly funeral, I have withheld identification because to do otherwise would be insensitive. The stories however are true and the omission of names does not take from their authenticity nor from their value.

During my childhood I spent many happy days in the house of my widowed aunt, Delia Fitzpatrick in Garryedmond, which is situated about four miles east of Claremorris, where she lived with her two sons and her daughter. The boys were excellent violinists and in the late Summer evenings, often after a hard day's work, Jack would take down the violin and play while sitting on the wall outside the house. He played reels, jigs and hornpipes with abandon, and although his attempts to make a musician out of me failed abysmally I can remember the names of many of the tunes which he tried to teach me including *The Boys of Blue Hill, Lanigan's Ball, The Three Little Drummers,* and *The Connacht Man's Ramble*. The last named provided me with a cue for the title of my book.

My story is based largely in my native Garryedmond and its adjoining townlands and on people with whose customs and lifestyle I was familiar. But people of similar background and tradition would be found in almost any part of rural Ireland and the same scenario would apply to their activities, interests and pastimes.

As a member of the Mayo Association in Galway I went on many archaeological and historical tours throughout the West. The tours were conducted at various times by Etienne Rynne, Professor of Archaeology, U.C.G. and by two eminent writers and historians from Galway R.T.C., namely Peadar O'Dowd, a native Galwegian and Bernard O'Hara who hails from Killasser near Swinford. Our trips included visits to monastic ruins, museums and archaeological sites as well as former workhouses and the remains of other historical buildings. On itineraries through Mayo there were halts at Shrule, Ballinrobe, Ballinasmalla, Knock, Kiltimagh, Killasser, Mayo Abbey, Ballintubber and the five thousand year old Ceide Fields near Ballycastle. In addition to the guided tours and interesting talks given by tour leaders there are many visitor centres where films, books and exhibits are devoted to helping people to learn about the type of dress worn, the age of excavated stones and uncovered ruins, the method of farming, the manner of cooking and generally describing what life was like in our island all those centuries ago.

Following some of these tours it occurred to me that the members of my own family never saw a limekiln burning, corn being threshed with a flail or even by a threshing mill, a cow milked by hand nor a thatcher working at his trade. They never witnessed a vagrant tramping the dusty sand roads nor have they any idea of what a cattle fair was like. Neither did they witness a politician standing on a wall outside a church expounding his views on how the country should be governed while running the gauntlet of hecklers. They did not endure the primitiveness of living without the benefit of running water and electricity, but neither did they experience the enjoyment of seeing neighbours gathered around a warm turf fire on a Winter night sharing their views and discussing their simple adventures.

We are getting experts to dig deeper into history and archaeology and while interested sight-seers visit museums and various historic sites around the country, we may be ignoring present-day trends and peculiarities and allowing the mundane occurrences of the immediate past to fall into oblivion.

Should anybody feel tempted to scoff at those who grew up in the times and situations described they would do well to ponder on the fact that they themselves are only a generation or two removed from these conditions. Over the past fifty years the alterations in the pace of life and conditions of work which have taken place in rural Ireland have exceeded the combined changes of the previous half millennium. But although people nowadays have most of the hard work done by machinery they seem to have less time for conversation with their neighbours, and the social aspect of working at the thresher and putting in the hay has faded into antiquity.

As there is a danger that a way of life will soon be past recall, I have decided to record some of the common events of my early life that by now have become part of our history. Most of the occurrences have been witnessed by me and I am satisfied concerning the authenticity of the incidents told to me by people now gone to their rest who were of a generation before mine. I have taken the liberty of describing some of my neighbours, and in detailing stories about them and traits that characterised them it is my hope that I have succeeded in doing justice to all. Like the inhabitants of the Blasket Islands who were so aptly described by Tomás Ó Crohan in his book *The Islandman*, the like of them will never be seen again.

It is my fervent hope that this book will reach many of the countless friends I have made throughout a lifetime, and bring back happy memories to those who shared with me the many episodes recalled.

Sé mo ghuí go daingean go mbeidh fáil ar an leabhar seo ag na céadta cáirde a ndearna mé teagmháil leo i rith mo shaoil.
Tá súil agam go dtabharfaidh sé chun cuimhne dóibh a lán des na heachtraí atá luaite anseo.
Go dtuga Dia solas na bhFlaitheas dóibh siúd díobh atá imithe ar shlí na fírinne.
Agus dom' léitheoiri uilig tá súil agam go mbainfidh siad an oiread taitnimh as a léamh is a bhain mise as a scríobh.

1

Historical Notes

LANDLORDISM AND ITS AFTERMATH

Garryedmond is the Anglicised form of Garraí Éamoinn which means The Garden of Edmond. It was called after Edmond Burke (Éamonn de Búrca) who became landlord of the townland in the mid eighteenth century. Most landlords farmed a goodly portion of their lands themselves and the remainder they rented out in holdings of about fifteen to twenty acres to tenants. Each holding had a thatched dwelling house and farm buildings and the tenant had to pay an agreed rent to the landlord. Edmond Burke did not farm any land in Garryedmond as he lived with his family at Oldtown near Irishtown which place later became the cradle of the Land League. Consequently there was no landlord's residence or "big house" in Garryedmond unlike our neighbouring townlands of Caraun and Cloontooa.

The last of the landlords in Cloontooa were the Trestons, and their descendant, Noel Treston, today occupies the house and he farms the lands which have been in the family possession for several generations.

In the heyday of the landlords the townland of Caraun was owned by the Trenchs. The last of that family to reside there was John Trench who was known locally as "Mr. John," and he died about 1920, when landlordism was fast becoming a memory. As he was unmarried and had no legitimate heir, his own family farm, which included the big house, passed on to his nephew Richard Prendergast who was his sister's eldest son. The latter was born and reared in England where he was working as a commercial representative at the time of Mr. John's death.

Although Mr. John was unmarried he was the father of a number of children with a local girl named Peggy, who lived close to the big house where she had been a maid from her girlhood. The children were christened in the name of Trench and were reared in Caraun. When he was dying Mr. John wished to leave his property to his eldest son, Richard Trench, who was better known as "Dick". However it was what was known as "blood property." This meant that it could be inherited only by a blood descendant but as Dick was born out of wedlock he was not legally entitled to it. He had Trench blood in his veins, but illegitimate children, as they were described at the time, had no standing in law.

Practically all the neighbours wished to see Dick Trench inherit the property but there was nothing they could do about it. Their liberal attitude seems quite remarkable for an era when people held very conservative views on morality and it said much for Dick's popularity and standing in the community. However he was forced to leave Caraun and, having married a Ballyhaunis girl, they settled in her home town where they raised three children. His son, also Richard, was personally known to me and I met him regularly when I worked in Ballyhaunis where he owned and collected the customs.

On the death of Mr. John, his nephew Richard Prendergast arrived from England and he took possession of the house and lands. He was accompanied by his brother John and their father Michael. For a time the local people referred to him as "*the young heir.*"

Richard's father was born in the townland of Caraun but in a house on another farm which was later purchased by Ned Byrne and occupied by him and his family for over fifty years until his death in 1987. Michael Prendergast had married Mr. John's sister and they emigrated to England where he became a policeman. He had retired and his wife was dead by the time he returned to Ireland when Richard succeeded to Caraun House and the family farm.

Among my earliest memories of growing up in my humble Garryedmond home are those of local people visiting in our house all the year round but especially during the long Winter nights. I particularly remember the visits of Richard Prendergast who by then was being described as "the landlord." He stands out in my mind because in many ways he was unlike our other neighbours. When I first knew him he was approaching middle age, erect in bearing and his manner and behaviour were at all times most gentlemanly. His pronounced English accent was unique in our district and a black bowler hat was a regular part of his attire. He was a chain smoker, so much so that his small trim moustache, which should have been much the same grey as his hair, was singed to a burnt brown except at the extreme outer edges.

John was more of an intellectual than Richard. Well educated, widely read and capable of discussing philosophy, theology and many facets of science, he was a great conversationalist but found few locally to whom he could relate. While living in Caraun he wrote a novel, giving it the title "*A Traveller's Tale*", but so far as I know, the work was never published.

Michael died shortly after they settled in Ireland. His death was due indirectly to the turbulent political situation existing here at the time. The civil war was at its height and one night a group of Republicans 'acquired' his motor car for use as a quick getaway after a bank raid. It was taken from a shed near the lower avenue gates and was found abandoned not many miles distant by the Free State soldiers a few days later and duly returned.

Believing that an attempt would be made to steal it again for a similar errand he put a strong lock on the shed door and proceeded to install a window in the gable of the dwelling house overlooking it. Should his expectation be realised the contents of a shotgun would be used on the intruders.

It would have been a wiser decision to have had a garage built underneath the existing window of his bedroom, because he spent several days in very cold weather hacking out a large hole in the wide stone gable wall. He never achieved his objective because, as a result of the very harsh weather and his own poor constitution, he got pneumonia from which he died within days.

Richard, John and their housekeeper Bridget Flannery, a native of Cloontooa, continued to live in the big house. The window was never installed and the hole was eventually filled in. It was so roughly patched up that on the outside of the gable visible evidence of its existence remained.

Many generations of the Trenchs had been landlords of Caraun and as approximately half of our holding was in that townland they had jurisdiction over it. Some landlords believed in keeping their tenants subdued, and they would not allow them to carry out even the smallest of improvements to their houses without permission. If tenants did anything against the will of the landlord they were liable to be evicted. All houses were of standard size and of the same design. Each had a kitchen, two bedrooms, a "hag" (a bed built into the wall) and a loft and was roofed with thatch. The size of the windows, the height of the doors and indeed every single feature was decided by the landlord. If he did give permission to have beneficial alterations made he would in all probability then increase the rent and if the tenant objected or was unable to pay, he was evicted. Tenants were required to work gratis for the landlord whenever he requested and even if they had hay ready for saving or corn shedding for want of harvesting they had to attend to the landlord's requirements. Refusal would mean eviction so there was no refusal. Within their territory all the land, turbary, dwelling houses and outoffices were in the ownership of the landlords, as were fishing and shooting rights.

Apparently the Trestons, the Trenchs, and the Burkes were "good" landlords. There is no record of them browbeating their tenants or unfairly evicting any of them. Several generations of Costellos survived in our own holding since they first arrived from Aghamore and it is still in our family possession.

By the time Richard Prendergast came to Caraun the power of the landlord had vanished. Despite the local support for Dick Trench the neighbours, by and large, welcomed the young heir. Every Summer the former tenants who, thanks mainly to Michael Davitt, founder of the Land League, were now the owners of their holdings, gave him a day putting in hay. My father was among them and at an early age I once accompanied him. It was my first experience of a meitheal. There were about twelve men plus Richard and John engaged in the task and although they were city born and reared the Prendergast brothers were just as capable at farming as their Irish neighbours.

By modern standards Caraun House was not big but by comparison with those of the local tenant farmers it was a mansion. It stood two storeys high and had a slated roof. A fenced off tree-lined avenue from the public road to a landlord's residence was almost a necessary status symbol. A road about ten feet wide ran in the centre and along each side of it were grass margins up to thirty feet wide. At the entrance were large iron gates hanging on ornate pillars. A wealthy landlord was likely to have a gate lodge built adjacent to the entrance and occupied by the family of one of his employees. The man would be employed as a farm labourer or a gardener and it would be his wife's duty to act as gatekeeper for the landlord and his family when they were driving through.

Caraun House had no gate lodge but there was an avenue which is still there. However, it was designed in a most unusual way for it did not lead directly to the house but instead ran by it. Some two hundred yards beyond the house the grass margin ceased but the road continued into a cul de sac and it served the occupants of four other houses.

The Prendergasts often had cattle and sheep grazing on the avenue margins and to prevent them from straying, there were heavy iron gates placed at the entrance to and exit from the avenue. These gates were always closed across the road and the members of the four households had to dismount from their carts, traps or bicycles every time they went in and out the roadway. This was very troublesome for them and on several occasions they requested "the landlord" to fence off the margins and remove the gates. He refused to do so and their benevolent attitude towards him underwent a dramatic change and a period of antagonism and feuding commenced. In the darkness of a night the pillars were flattened and the gates were carried off and dumped in a nearby ditch. The incident was reported to the gárdaí who came out to investigate the matter. They found the gates without difficulty and Richard had the pillars rebuilt and the gates were hung again. He then made a claim for malicious damage against the Co. Council for the destruction of the pillars and he was awarded compensation. When the Council paid compensation in a malicious damage claim they placed a levy on the ratepayers of that district to recoup it, so in reality it was themselves and their neighbours who paid for the restoration. Following advice from a legal expert that no compensation was payable for property stolen, as distinct from what was maliciously damaged, a new strategy was decided upon. Within a

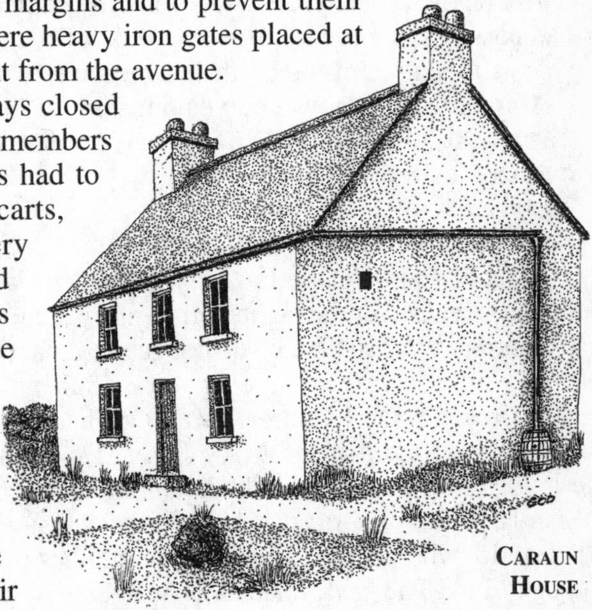

CARAUN HOUSE

short time the gates disappeared but there was no interference with the pillars. So well were they hidden that they were never seen again except by those involved in their disposal. The removal of the gates was a victory for the householders as they now had the freedom to walk, cycle or drive to and from their homes without hindrance.

Richard sold the farm shortly afterwards and he returned to England where he died some years later. Both his brother and their housekeeper had passed away earlier. He had lived in Caraun for more than twenty years and neither of the brothers ever married.

Caraun House, now empty and forlorn, is in the possession of local farmer, Jimmy Cunnane, and still stands boldly on the hilltop overlooking most of the townland.

COSTELLO GENEALOGY

The Costellos came to Garryedmond from the Aghamore district towards the end of the eighteenth century. Unfortunately the records in Claremorris Parish Church do not go back that far and the first recorded birth in the family is that of my grandfather, John, who was born on 10th June 1842. His parents were Michael and Brigid Costello (nee Canavan). John married Mary Jordan from Rookfield, Knock, in the old Claremorris Church which was situated where the town hall now stands, on 12th February, 1863. The best man was his brother, Michael Costello, who was the maternal grandfather of Paddy, May, John and Peggy Foy. The bridesmaid was Margaret Webb, but as in the case of my great grandmother, I have not succeeded in getting any information about her. An interesting item recorded in connection with the marriage of John and Mary Costello was the offering given of one pound, fourteen shillings and six pence. It was also of interest that my grandfather was married at the early age of twenty one. They had nine children the eldest of whom was born on 31st January, 1864 and the youngest on 4th February 1883.

McMANUS GENEALOGY

On my mother's side my great grandfather was Michael McManus of Koilmore. He was married to Nan O'Donnell and one of their children was my grandfather, Jimmy McManus. Jimmy married Bridget Nally from Mayo Abbey and they had eleven children, of whom my mother Rose McManus was the second youngest. A son and a daughter died of scarlet fever while they were only in their teens. A daughter, Delia, married Michael Fitzpatrick of Garryedmond and they had three children. A son, John, remained in the home place in Koilmore and he married Mary Begley of Carrowbeg. They had two daughters, Delia, who married Joe Johnston from Reisk and Margaret who married Paddy Stephens from Meelickmore.

Margaret Stephens, Meelickmore, her children and grandchildren, Kevin Johnston, Koilmore, his sister Claire Robinson, Aghamore, and her family, Michael Fitzpatrick, solicitor, Listowel, my brother, John, and myself with our children and grandchildren are direct descendants of Jimmy and Bridget McManus. We are the only ones living in Ireland but there must be hundreds in America with whom we never had contact.

My maternal grandfather Jimmy McManus, was a quack dentist. My mother often talked about the numerous people who came to their house, some from considerable distances, to have teeth extracted by him. How he acquired whatever skill he possessed in this domain I do not know. He used some type of pincer or plier – it would scarcely be called a forceps – but there was no anaesthetic and the mouthwash was lukewarm salted water. Luckily none of his "patients" ever got blood-poisoning.

It is regrettable that most people do not become interested in their family history until they are advanced in years. Perhaps my efforts may inspire others to trace their own family histories for at least a few generations back. I hope too that my family, my brother's family and their children will be interested in genealogy and that this short record will be of some encouragement to them. There is now a genealogical research centre in Ballinrobe known as "South Mayo Family Research" and for a small fee they will trace as far as is humanly possible the details of any family history from the southern part of the county.

A NORMAN FAMILY

The Costellos were a Norman family who arrived with the invaders in the twelfth century. Like other conquerors I presume that they did their share of plundering although there is no evidence to this effect. They settled in East Mayo and spread out from there. Whatever about their foreign origin, like many of their race, they became more Irish than the Irish themselves.

The following is an extract from *Irish Families* by Edward MacLysaght: *"The Costelloes were originally Nangles, or de Angulos, as that great Norman family was called when, soon after the invasion, the Anglo-Normans occupied Connacht. The first reference to them in the Four Masters is in the year 1193 when they were called the sons of Oistealb, who was a son of the famous Gilbert de Nangle, whence was formed the surname Mac Oisdealbh, later Mac Oisdealbhaigh, anglice Mac Costello. It is the first recorded instance of a Norman family assuming a Mac name. Thenceforward they became thoroughly Irish. There are many traditional tales of the feuds between the MacCostelloes and MacDermots: none more poignant than the tragic love story of Una, daughter of Charles MacDermot (the last inagurated chieftain of that name), and the son of the head of the MacCostello family, who lie in adjoining graves beside the ruins of the church on Trinity Island. Their lands were in Co. Mayo and the barony of Costello, in the east of that county, was named from the MacCostelloes who possessed it up to the end of the sixteenth century. In 1565 their chief seat was near Ballaghadereen, which is now included in Co. Roscommon. The name Costello (the Mac has been entirely dropped) is found to-day chiefly in Counties Mayo and Galway."*

They founded the Augustinian Friary in Ballyhaunis in 1348 and Urlaur Abbey for the Dominicans in 1434. Urlaur has been in ruins since the Cromwellian times but Saint Mary's in Ballyhaunis is still thriving and it is prominently displayed on a placard at the entrance gates that it was founded by Jordan Dubh Mac Costello.

The family that came to Garryedmond were weavers as were the Foys who arrived much later from near Westport, and some generations of their descendants continued with that business along with farming. The Foys were the last family in the area to surrender the craft, but their descendants occupy the original homestead to this day. There were two intermarriages between the Foys and the Costellos in the last generation so the surviving members of the two families are related.

FROM THE DIRT TRACK TO THE HIGHWAY

Roads as we now know them replaced dirt tracks, and when they were first made and fenced off, the townland boundaries which were the usual extent of the landlords' property, and the mearings between the tenants' holdings were already in place. In order to lose only the minimum of their own lands when the roads were being built, the landlords insisted on the principal thoroughfares running as far as possible along by their boundaries, and the tenants did likewise regarding the lesser roads. In this way, half the land was taken from each owner or occupier through whose property they ran. Frequently the boundaries were winding and the result was winding or crooked roads.

The cost of making the roads was borne by the authorities which in effect was the British Government who controlled the Rural District Councils which preceded the County Councils. The workers were quite pleased with the system because if the roads were to be crooked it would take longer to make them and this in turn would make more work available near their homes.

An interesting incident took place when the road entering Caraun from Garryedmond at the Blessed Well was being built. The mearing between the townlands was a stream, but as the new road was giving no service to anybody in Garryedmond, the route taken was entirely on the Caraun side until the wayside well was reached. There the stream veered to the right but instead of following it, the authorities made the last few yards of the new road straight out to meet the existing one at right angles. This was both sensible and practical. But in so doing they infringed a few feet into Burke property in Garryedmond. At that time the tenant of the Garryedmond holding, now owned by Michael Goggins, had no objection to it. However the agent for Landlord Burke had other ideas. He used the Courts and succeeded in forcing a change in the course of the road. That is the way it has remained to the present time leaving a sharp, dangerous corner. That episode took place during the lifetime of my grandfather.

Most roads in the West are now tarred or blacktopped but up to the nineteen eighties there were many byroads and access roads still sand surfaced and some had not yet been taken over by the Local Authority. The people who used them had to repair and maintain them or else endure the inconvenience of potholes.

In the part of Garryedmond where I lived and which long ago was called Laghera there were four houses. The road was a cul de sac and it had to be maintained by the residents until it was taken over by the County Council in 1965. All the able-bodied men in the four houses spent about three consecutive days each year cutting the bushes and briars along the fences and giving it a liberal dressing of sand supplied free of charge by John Foy who had a sandpit nearby from which it was transported by ass and cart.

Roads were tarred for the first time in Mayo in 1924 and it was many years afterwards before all the main roads in the county were so surfaced. Among those selected in the earlier stages was the main road leading from Westport towards Dublin and running through Castlebar, Claremorris and Ballyhaunis. The Department of Local Government, now the The Department of the Environment have since altered the description of some of the main roads and the portion from Castlebar going through the aforementioned towns was changed to secondary status.

The road from Drimneen to Brickens running through Ballinasmalla, Cartownacross and Garryedmond was first tarred in 1966.

RAILWAYS AND SLATES

The laying of the railway, which runs through Garryedmond and Cloontooa from Dublin to Westport, was completed in the eighteen sixties and it was subsequently extended to Mulranny and Achill. My grandfather, John Costello, worked on its construction as did most of the young men in the district. It was known as The Midland & Great Western Railway and a public notice displayed at level crossings, warning of the imposition of fines if gates were left open, bore that heading. The gatehouse, as the gate minder's lodge at the level crossing was called was erected in conjunction with the laying of the railway and it was the first, and for many decades the only slated house in Garryedmond.

In Koilmore the school residence was the lone slated dwelling house while in Ballyglass and Ballykinave the long defunct Congested Districts Board, the forerunner of The Irish Land Commission, had divided farms of land into small holdings on which they built one storey slated houses. Most of them are standing today, still occupied but renovated and vastly improved by each succeeding generation. There is no trace of a thatched house anywhere in the vicinity now.

RURAL ELECTRIFICATION

Generating stations provided electricity in limited areas from the end of the nineteenth century, but the introduction of the Shannon

Scheme in 1927 was the first move to supply it countrywide. By the early thirties almost every town of any significance was connected. So it surprised me when I went to work as a shop assistant in Ballinasloe in 1946, to find that, although there was electricity in the houses and factories, the street lighting was still supplied by gaslight. It was fascinating to watch the lamp lighter cycle from lamp post to lamp post carrying a staff which looked much like the handle of a hay rake. Cycling to the edge of the footpath and stopping directly beneath the lamp, he placed one foot on the path while remaining astride. He then raised the staff upright towards the lamp on which there must have been some kind of a switch. Apparently there was a fitting on the top of the staff which he inserted into the switch before giving it a little pull. A weak light appeared in the lamp which gradually grew stronger until there was a reasonable flame. The operation took only a couple of seconds and he flitted on to the next lamp post. There were no street lights after midnight and although I never saw him turning them off I presume that he did the rounds again to quench them.

It was not until World War II was over that plans were made to extend electricity to rural Ireland. It took a couple of years to take off and strangely, rural dwellers gave it a mixed welcome. One would expect that areas would be vying with each other to be first. But the opposite was the case, in many places.

Well attended meetings were held in every rural parish, usually spearheaded by the local priest who was always in favour of getting it. He would have many reasons for favouring installation. Firstly it would bring many progressive benefits to his parish and extra personal comforts to his parishioners. Secondly, he would avail of these comforts himself for his house, his Church and the schools of which he was sole manager. Thirdly, although unlikely to be affluent he was equally unlikely to be over-worried about having to find the money to pay the bi-monthly bill for rental and power consumed. In the villages the business and professional people were in favour of installation but farmers treated the proposal with caution.

The parishioners of Knock were among the earliest applicants for a supply. Because of its international shrine the E.S.B. were prepared to give the area priority provided that there were enough applicants and there was a very positive response from Knock residents. Father John Colleran was rector of St. Colman's College in Claremorris at the time and he decided to press a case for a supply to his institution in conjunction with the installation in Knock. He called a meeting in the college to which all residents for miles around were invited as well as a representative from the E.S.B.

The latter explained the procedure for installation and he gave an estimate of costs. These would vary from house to house as they were based on the size of the dwelling and outoffices. Two people from each townland were delegated by the meeting to visit every household in their own area and canvass them to accept it because unless there was a reasonable percentage of applicants the Board would not go ahead with any installation in that area.

The canvassers returned from Cartownacross, Knockatubber, Caraun, Garryedmond and Cloontooa districts with a negative response. This result was partly due to some canvassers being against acceptance themselves and partly to counteractive advice from business people in the town. But the main reason was that farmers at the time feared that they would be unable to keep up the payments for rental and electricity consumed.

Fortunately a sufficient number of householders in the vicinity signed for acceptance to justify a supply to the college as well as to Knock and to all who applied for it along by that road. Sixteen years elapsed before a supply was offered again in the areas where it had been rejected but on this occasion there was no refusal.

Long before the advent of the Shannon Scheme there were a few enterprising local people who generated their own electricity. The Gilmore family in Brickens harnessed the river running by their home and provided light and power for their own area. Edward Griffith generated electricity with a diesel engine in Ballindine and he supplied direct current to many householders in that village. In Knockatubber, Michael McHugh had a windcharger which was erected by his brother-in-law, Michael Reidy, who had a very inventive mind.

PIPED WATER

Nearly every household in the country has piped water today and it is difficult to believe that the first group water supply scheme in Mayo was not installed until the nineteen sixties. One of the first, if not the first, was in Garryduff near Ballindine and great credit was due to the innovation of the residents as well as to the engineer, Gerry McLoughlin, who played a primary role in its provision. Strange to relate there was a small measure of opposition from a couple of people living in the townland but the reason was not financial but political and it quickly fizzled out.

The Knockatubber Group Water Scheme which supplies four townlands was installed in the nineteen seventies. The source is a spring in Garryedmond now known as Tobar Mhuire but when I was living there it was always referred to as "The Blessed Well."

Before the advent of group schemes a concrete tank adjoined almost every house into which rain water flowed through a downpipe from the roof during wet weather. Our wet climate ensured that there was usually enough water in the tank for domestic washing and for boiling potatoes and vegetables, but it was not fit for human consumption. Therefore drinking water had to be carried in buckets from spring wells, and in our district most people were lucky enough to have one near their homes.

When new houses were built large concrete tanks, having a capacity of not less than three thousand gallons, were erected close by. This was the minimum size accepted by the Department of Local Government before they agreed to give a grant towards the installation of water. The water had to be pumped by hand into a small tank in the attic whence it had a gravity flow to the kitchen sink, the bath and toilet. The system is the same today except that it now fills automatically.

WATER DIVINERS

Drinking water had still to be procured from a well and there were some farms where there was no such facility so they had to bore into the ground for a supply. The service of a water diviner was used to locate a spring which could be more than one hundred feet beneath the surface.

For many years it was my pleasure to work with Pat Duane of Castlebar when I was an insurance agent. Combined with being an excellent insurance man Pat was also a gifted water diviner and on numerous occasions I watched in fascination as he obliged farmers by finding springs for them. He used a Y shaped hazel rod of about eighteen inches in length, and he held the upper portions very tightly, one in each hand, while the stem pointed straight out in front of him. If after walking the length of a garden or field he failed to find a spring he would move crosswise. He would step field after field until a spot was reached where the rod told him that there was a spring underneath. I never saw him to fail but he told me that he, or rather the farmers, had some disappointments in other parts of the county.

When he arrived over the spring the stem of the rod which was pointing directly forward, suddenly turned downwards, sometimes with great force. He walked around that area until he found the exact spot where it was strongest and from the strength of the pressure on the rod he could judge almost exactly the depth at which water could be found. Having marked the spot, the farmer then employed a professional well borer who had special equipment for the purpose, and who having reached the water, installed a pump, which he connected by a pipe to the source.

I once took the rod in my hands and walked over the spot where he had found a spring but there was no movement. However when Pat put his hands over mine and held them tightly the stem again turned downwards with such force as to nearly take the skin off my palms.

Pat accepted that water divining was a gift from God and he had no idea how he came to have it. As a mere boy he accidentally discovered his rare talent which he generously shared with anybody who requested it.

Pat Duane's father-in-law was the late Sean Langan of Castlebar who was a noted teacher, lecturer, and Irish language enthusiast who, in his leisure time, organised Feiseanna throughout Connacht. He played an impressive and generous role in keeping our native culture and traditions alive in the West of Ireland. An employee of Mayo Vocational Education Committee he taught Irish classes for many years in the old town hall in Claremorris.

THE HEDGE SCHOOLS

My grandfather went to a hedge school but that did not mean that he studied under a hedge. Hedge schools had come some distance from the penal days when any kind of schooling was illegal for Catholics and when classes were in fact held in makeshift shelters or hovels and during the Summer out by hedges and fences while "students" took turns to act as sentries in case they were caught by the authorities. Like the priest who was also the teacher on occasions, the schoolmaster had a price on his head. Those who gave them shelter or sent their children to hedge schools were also at risk and when discovered they faced severe fines, imprisonment and sometimes they were exiled to the colonies. The authorities at that time believed, probably with some justification, that it was easier to keep subdued an ignorant and uneducated people than a populace with learning.

Early in the nineteenth century the laws against education and against Catholicism generally were relaxed. Hedge schools were no longer illegal and classes were held in houses but the old description remained. The authorities were in no rush to build schools and staff them but nuns, priests and brothers came to the rescue supplying buildings and teachers. In today's affluent and secular society, their work and the sacrifices they made are not appreciated or even remembered.

They however could only do so much and even after the Government erected and staffed school buildings, hedge schools continued. At least at that stage they were not forced to assemble in secrecy by hedges or in hovels. The teachers' renumeration came from the parents who paid whatever they could afford and that was never very much.

I have no idea what house contained the hedge school which my grandfather attended nor do I know the names of his teachers. But neighbours accepted him to be an educated man and many of them requested his assistance with paper work such as writing letters on their behalf. He got newspapers regularly and his reading aloud of news and reports was eagerly awaited by his illiterate and semi-illiterate neighbours as they visited around his fireside at night. His wife, who was my grandmother, like most of her contemporaries could neither read nor write.

THE NATIONAL SCHOOLS

Time passed and eventually the State (meaning the British Government) took total responsibility for primary education, building residences for teachers as well as school-houses in the process. That may have suggested a change of heart on their part but it also gave them an opportunity to undermine the Irish language. Had we not achieved the freedom of twenty six counties following The War of Independence they would have succeeded in their efforts to obliterate it.

Prior to 1926 the system of training national teachers was very different from what it is today. James Murphy, my teacher in Koilmore, often told us that his teaching career commenced when he was fourteen years of age. In his day pupils interested in becoming teachers advised the school principal of their intentions before they had completed the national school curriculum. This would be towards the end of their year in seventh class when they would be about fourteen years of age. The principal advised the school manager and consequently an inspector from the Department of Education and another official from the training college called to examine and assess the candidates. If the aspirants were found to be suitable and provided they could be accommodated in the school, arrangements were made to have them kept on as monitors or monitresses. It was in fact a type of apprenticeship. They taught in the school for three years under the supervision of the principal who sent regular reports on their progress to the inspectors. At the end of that time an examination took place and if successful they entered a training college for a three year training course. There was another examination at the end of the training and those who were successful were then accepted as trained teachers and were admissible for employment in any national school in the country. Most boys from the West of Ireland were trained in Saint Patrick's College, Drumcondra while most girls were trained in Carysfort. There were also training colleges in Waterford and Limerick.

Garryedmond born Margaret Walsh (nee Foy), who for many years taught in Cultibo school, was one of those who made her teaching debut in Koilmore. Her cousin, Luke Foy, also from Garryedmond, was a monitor there too but unfortunately he died while training in St. Patricks.

In 1926, Ernest Blythe the Minister for Education introduced the preparatory examination which supplanted the monitorial system. His main purpose was to revive Irish. On completing the national school curriculum, prospective teachers now sat for this examination and if they were successful they entered preparatory colleges such as Coláiste Caoimhín in Glasnevin or Coláiste Éinne in Galway for a four year course at the end of which they got the Leaving Certificate if successful. They all had to be proficient in Irish. The Leaving Certificate course was also available in several other educational establishments but each of those who obtained it in the preparatory colleges had the great advantage of being guaranteed a place in a training college. That course then took two years and the first batch of preparatory pupils entered Coláiste Caoimhín in 1927 and were trained in 1932.

CASTLEMACGARRETT

THE CASTLE

Castlemacgarrett, situated a short distance from Claremorris on the Galway road, was as its name suggests, a castle. Built in 1694 by Geoffrey Browne and the home of the Browne family for centuries, it was taken over by the Land Commission in the mid nineteen sixties. Many years ago a portion was burned down in an accidental fire but it was quickly restored.

The last of the Brownes to own the castle was the only Lord Oranmore that I knew. Although a good and generous employer who occasionally hosted parties for the employees in the castle he still kept them at a distance. They were often heard referring to him reverently as "his lordship" whether talking among themselves or to outsiders. There were stories told that when he cycled along the miles of sand roads running through the two thousand acre estate, some workers in the nearby fields stood to attention and raised their caps in salute.

In all large estates like Breaffy House, Ashford Castle, Castlemacgarrett and others there were many gamekeepers employed. Generally known to be most diligent in their duties where trespassers were concerned, they did not hesitate to report even their best friends when the latter were caught poaching. There were sportsmen, however, who believed that their lordships and squireships should not have these rights because they claimed that the forebears of all the landed gentry had acquired their possessions wrongfully, so they had no problem, where conscience or morality was concerned, in making raids on the plentiful stocks of game.

A well known barber in Claremorris once told me that he was cycling, complete with gun, ammunition and bag, by one of these estates when he spotted a fine cock pheasant within shooting distance of the road. He raised his gun and shot the bird. Having dallied for a while he climbed over the wall and entered the field to retrieve the prize. However when lifting it from the grass, a gamekeeper who was also a close acquaintance, appeared from a concealed position in the nearby bushes and deprived him of it.

Within a few days a letter arrived from the nobleman summoning him to his office. On his appearance he was ordered to pay a fine of one pound and give an undertaking never again to set foot inside those hallowed walls. It was his belief that the imposition of the fine was illegal, but feeling so happy to have the matter settled he willingly paid it. It is less sure that he never returned.

Of course gamekeepers had duties other than catching poachers. They helped in breeding game birds and nurturing them to maturity when their lordships with their friends, usually from overseas, had the pleasure of shooting them without any fear of being fined. They were paid small wages but they also got a commission for every undesirable predatory bird or animal they shot. For example a shot magpie might realise three pence, a hawk could be worth a shilling and a rat six or seven pence.

Apart from those working on the farm and looking after game, Lord Oranmore gave good employment in the saw-mills. Also employed at the castle were cooks, laundry workers, chauffeurs, lorry drivers, valets and chambermaids. Houses were provided on the estate for many of his employees and generation after generation of the same families found work in the castle and on the lands. He often paid the medical bills for employees and their spouses before there were compulsory national health benefits and decades before the advent of the Voluntary Health Insurance Scheme.

He was a great entertainer and apart from the elite who regularly attended the annual "shoot" which lasted a week, there were many other notable people known to visit the castle including Erskine Childers, who later became President of Ireland.

When the Land Commission decided to purchase Castlemacgarrett they put a value on it which was not acceptable to Lord Oranmore and Browne. On appeal to the Courts he succeeded in getting a substantial increase and the sale went ahead and a ceremonial take over was arranged at the castle.

As a public representative at the time, an invitation to attend was sent to me by the office of the Minister for Lands. A large gathering of invited people was present from all walks in life. The Minister, Míceál Ó Móráin, was accompanied by officials from his Department and the Land Commission was represented by its Chief Inspector, Bekan born Dick Tarpey, and by Con Kelly and Kevin Cowley. Legal people from both sides attended to witness the handing over to the Minister of a neat little sod taken from the ground which symbolised the transfer of ownership of the land. He was then presented with the key of the castle. A crew from R.T.E. was present with cameras and a report was transmitted on the news programme that night so we all appeared on television. After the ceremony, we attended a reception hosted by the Department in the Western Hotel, Claremorris, which was owned by Christina O'Toole, a native of Louisburgh and sister of Martin Joe O'Toole who later had a distinguished career in both the Dáil and the Seanad. (Incidentally Martin Joe has the unique distinction of being the only person ever to serve on Mayo County Council for an unbroken period of forty years. To mark the occasion he was honoured by his colleagues with a civic reception and presentation in June 1995). A short time later, the Land Commission offered the castle for sale with somewhat less than one hundred acres of land adjoining it. The people of Claremorris were hopeful that whoever purchased the magnificent building would put it to use beneficial to the community. They feared that if purchased by foreign speculators it might be allowed to deteriorate or even be pulled down as it was understood to have very valuable accessories such as dismountable ceilings and gates. The Sisters of Our Lady of the Apostles, who had a house in Cork, were known to be interested in acquiring it and virtually everybody in the locality strongly supported them. A difficulty was that no Religious Order could set up house in any diocese without the approval of the resident bishop, and the then Archbishop of Tuam, Most Reverend Doctor Walsh, was very reluctant to give permission. A small group of local people requested a meeting with him while he was on a visitation to Claremorris parish.

Having agreed to meet them in the presbytery he listened to their case on behalf of the Sisters but the result was an outright refusal.

Claremorris Chamber of Commerce under their President Tom McLoughlin then organised a large meeting of interested people in the Western Hotel, the purpose of which was to put pressure on the Archbishop to give permission. The hotel was crowded as many came from Ballyhaunis, Knock, Kiltimagh and Ballinrobe as well as Claremorris. This time the homework was done and a representative delegation was sent to Tuam. The members obviously impressed the Archbishop and the outcome was that permission was given which pleased all involved.

The auction took place in the premises of North's Auctioneers, in Dublin, and as a public representative I had the honour of being present. Accompanying me were Paddy McEllin, solicitor, representing the Sisters, Martin Finn, Co. Councillor and Arthur Hanley, a prominent businessman. Padraig Brennan, solicitor, was also there but he was representing another prospective purchaser.

There was much bidding at the auction and some confusion but anyway it was sold to the highest bidder and we were all satisfied with the end result that saw the Sisters as new owners of Castlemacgarrett. The price was less than twenty thousand pounds.

The castle was converted by them into a modern nursing home and throughout the intervening years they have done wonderful work in providing a home for the elderly to whom every comfort is given as well as the best in medical, physical and spiritual attention.

THE FIELDS

Modern farming methods have brought vast improvements in production, increased the wealth of the farmer and have made his work far less burdensome. But unfortunately they have also brought a certain amount of destruction in their wake. The introduction of silage which necessitates early cutting of grass in order to get two and sometimes three crops each year has taken away the habitat of the corncrake which species is now practically extinct in much of the country.

Enlarging the size of fields by converting four, five or more into one has resulted in the flattening of thousands of miles of sod fences and with them the virtual disappearance of furze and whitethorn which provided shelter and a measure of safety for the many small birds that nested in them. The sparrow family, the robin, greenfinch, yellow hammer, linnet and a host of others lost their usual haunts resulting in their numbers being considerably depleted, and some are facing extinction. Young children are consequently deprived of happy hours of searching for nests and comparing with their school friends the number they find. They have also been denied the pleasure of picking blackberries by the fences where briars once had a foothold.

Holdings have become much larger and in some places farmers have levelled all their sod fences replacing them with wire – usually electrified. The new method has facilitated "strip grazing" which is now regarded as essential for dairy farming and indeed for all types of livestock grazing. For tillage farmers too, the new system is beneficial because it has cut out much ground wastage and has presented them with the opportunity to increase or reduce the size of plots with little difficulty.

Historians will regret the disappearance of the small fields because they had their own distinct names, given for various reasons not always obvious now. We had just over twenty two acres in our holding and despite the fact that half of it was open or unfenced in the bog area we still had nine fields. Running by the public road was *The Acre* and it was known by this name to all our neighbours and passers by. Adjoining it was *The Big Park*. It was big by our standards but it contained less than five roods. Nearer the house we had *The Meadow Field* and *The Bog Garden*. The remainder had Irish names which made them far more interesting. They are listed as follows: *Páircín a' Lín* (the little field of the flax), *Páircín an Tobair* (the little field of the well), *Iomaire Bán* (the white ridge), *Poll Chéin* (Cian's hollow), and *Páircín na nGlas* (the little field of the greens or vegetables).

I knew the names of many of our neighbours' fields too. John Foy had *Cnocán Maicín* (the little hill of the quarrel), *Páirc Lamhnaigh* (Lowney's field), and *Lochán Liath* (the little grey pond or lake). He also had *Anthony's Field* which was purchased by his forebears from an Anthony Berry after whom they named it.

Flemings had *Sceithín* (the little bush), Peter Foy had *Cluain Each* (the meadow of the horse) and Keanes had *Súilín* (the little eye).

Prendergasts owned *Geata Beag* (the small gate), *Geata Bán* (the white gate), *Spadach* (the marsh), *Cluainín* (the little meadow), *Leac* (a layer of solid but easily broken mineral found about ten inches below the surface in some land). They also had part of *Lios Ard* (the high fort).

More than half of the fort, *Lios Ard*, was in Michael Foy's field which is now owned by his grandson Michael McGrath. It was believed that in earlier times stillborn children were interred in the fort when the Church would not allow the burial of unbaptised people in consecrated ground but this is only a legend for which there is no verification. The landscape of the West of Ireland is dotted with forts like *Lios Ard* which were built mainly in prehistoric times although some were constructed as late as the fifteenth century. Each fort was within sight of at least two others so that in the event of one being attacked a warning signal would be seen by the other two and a rescue operation could be mounted.

The names of the fields which I have listed are but a few of the many which were commonplace in and around Garryedmond and which are likely to become totally forgotten within a short time.

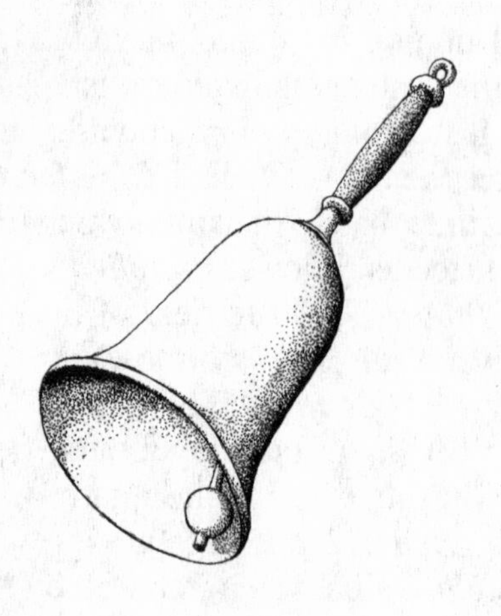

2

Some Early Memories

THE RIVER

Flowing along almost parallel to the railway line, ever increasing in measure as drains and minor streams discharged their waters to join the flow, and gently winding its way to a tributary of the Robe near Ballygowan, it was still only a rivulet although known to everybody as The River. That tributary was the nearest place where fish of any reasonable size could be caught but angling did not appeal to us or to any of our neighbours.

A stream which we called "The Main Drain," entered our land from Foy's and flowed on through Ruane's and Dunleavy's until it surged into "the river." Extensive drainage in the fifties dried a number of springs as well as draining the land so the amount of water there now is considerably less. Where it flowed through our land its bed was much lower than the ground surface above and at one point near a small bridge my father dug a wide opening down to the water on each side of the drain so that the cattle could reach it when they wanted to drink. He put a barrier of large stones across on the lower side, low enough for most of the water to flow over it but high enough to ensure that even in Summer there was a depth of over two feet leaving ample drinking water for the animals.

It was in this stream on a hot Summer day that I had my first experience of outdoor bathing. My brother, Séamus, and I sneaked to the stream carrying a towel and our Sunday pants under our arms. As with all rural boys at the time short pants were the norm, and during the Summer underclothes were discarded and being barefooted even going to school, all we had to take off were our shirts. Needless to say swimming togs were not items in our wardrobe, so we left on our old pants just in case somebody came along and we did not want to be seen in the nude. We stayed for only ten minutes or so in the water which as I can still recollect was very cold despite the day being uncomfortably warm.

We got out, dried ourselves and got into our Sunday pants and walked home, knowing that we would be caught out and expecting a good scolding from my mother. Strangely it did not materialise. She just told us to rinse the wet gear which we then hung across the nearby privet hedge to dry.

It was some years later before I had my first visit to the seaside and a real dip. My oldest brother had just purchased a new motor car and within a week he brought our whole family to Lecanvey. Afterwards we drove on to Louisburgh and on our return home we took in the Partry Mountains. For the next three years until the war situation forced private cars off the roads we had many trips to seaside places in Mayo, Sligo and Galway but the joy of that first outing so impressed me that to this day the area all around Clew Bay has a special appeal for me.

The wild beauty of Clew Bay and its hinterland entralls thousands of visitors and sightseers annually just as it captivated William Makepeace Thackeray in the mid-nineteenth century, when he visited Westport and the surrounding district. The following extract taken from *The Irish Sketch Book*, which he wrote in 1842, is just as relevant today for it is still largely unspoilt by man. "*And presently, from an eminence, I caught sight not only of a fine view, but of the most beautiful view I ever saw in the world, I think; and to enjoy the splendour of which I would travel a hundred miles in that car with that very horse and driver. The sun was just about to set, and the country round about and to the east was almost in twilight. The mountains were tumbled about in a thousand fantastic ways, and swarming with people. Trees, corn-fields, cottages, made the scene indescribably cheerful; noble woods stretched towards the sea, and abutting on them, between two highlands, lay the smoking town. Hard by was a large Gothic building – it is but a poor-house; but it looked like a grand castle in the grey evening. But the Bay – and the Reek which sweeps down to the sea – and a hundred islands in it, were dressed up in gold and purple and crimson, with the whole cloudy west in a flame. Wonderful, wonderful. . . ! The valleys in the road to Leenane have lost all glimpses of the sun ere this; and I suppose there is not a soul to be seen in the black landscape, or by the shores of the ghastly lakes, where the poor glass-blower from the whisky-shop is faintly travelling now."*

RACE MEETINGS

Sometime during those three years we drove to a race meeting in Milltown. It may not have had the status of the Galway or Listowel events but the enthusiasm of the punters, the air of hilarity and the excitement over the very fact of being there made it an occasion apart. It seems strange to have recounted memories before reaching my teen years but I remember comparing Milltown with a more classy meeting which I attended in Claremorris race-course some years earlier. Being very young my father took me with him in the donkey cart as far as Frank Clarke's house which was near the rear entrance to the Convent of Mercy. There we tethered the animal and we walked the short distance to the race-course. Because of my youth, racing did not mean anything to me but I relished the ancillary benefits of sweets and lemonade. We also enjoyed the tea and scones so generously provided by Mrs. Clarke before we tackled up the donkey and made our way home.

Partly because of the longer trip and in more comfortable transport, and perhaps because of being a few years older I found Milltown more enjoyable. Racing still meant little to me but the atmosphere which is unique to race meetings was easily perceived. Not much further knowledge of the sport has been gained by me in the intervening years, but I know that it brings immense joy and excitement into the lives of many people. Unfortunately it sometimes brings misery too.

Racing ceased in Claremorris many decades ago and all attempts to revive it failed. There are now a number of factories built on the grounds where there is also an all-weather running track but there is still hope that we will see racing in Claremorris again.

OUR FIRST RADIO

My brother, John, commenced studying in Dublin in 1930 and for six years he came home only for holidays at Christmas, Easter and Summer. Always having had an interest in electronics, wavelengths and kindred matters, he arrived one Christmas with a contraption described by him as a radio and purchased in some second-hand store in the capital. One would be forgiven for assuming that it was one of the first ever manufactured, it was so decrepit in appearance. A disadvantage was that it could be heard only through head-phones and therefore not more than one person at a time could listen in.

It was the first radio (although scarcely deserving to be so described) to appear in Garryedmond. A long outdoor aerial, which my father helped him to erect was required. A piece of the aerial wire was tied around the trunk of a sycamore tree about sixty feet from the house. After carefully knotting it, a small portion was left protruding and this was tied to an insulator. To the other side of the insulator was secured one end of the aerial proper which was then brought to the chimney where a similar insulating process took place. A lead was then brought down to the window and in through a small hole bored in the timber frame where it was connected to the apparatus. It appears that if the aerial directly touched either the tree or the chimney it would not intercept the waves and would therefore be useless.

The radio worked well and it was a source of great entertainment for us and it aroused curiosity among our visitors all of whom gratefully accepted a turn at the head-phones.

Within a few days a letter arrived from the postmaster in Claremorris addressed to my father advising him in very official language that it had come to his notice that a wireless receiving apparatus was installed in his premises and that under some Act of Parliament a licence for it was necessary. Because of our remote situation, speculation on who may have been the informer became a bigger topic of conversation among our visitors than was the radio itself.

My father must have paid the licence because the radio with the head-phones was part of our lives for a long time until it was replaced by another second-hand but more modern appliance.

MY FIRST VISIT TO THE TOWN

Six years of my life had passed before I had my first sight of our local town. Of course I was brought to the Parish Church to be baptised and to the doctor for the then compulsory vaccination against smallpox but those trips took place in the first weeks of my arrival in this world so I would not remember them.

I had heard so many tales from my older brother, Séamus, about the wonderful sights to be seen there that I longed to view them. He told me of wide streets almost half the width of some of our fields, footpaths where people walked while cars and lorries drove by, lights shining down at night from poles reaching half way to the sky, houses with most of them containing shops and all joined together having slated roofs and standing two and some three storeys high.

My young mind had difficulty in visualising such a scene and while yearning to go there, my feeling was that I would be unimpressed. The idea of people living in houses joined to others was almost repulsive to someone who had known only privacy and the freedom of large space around us.

On my arrival there however, I was not disappointed. In fact it far surpassed my dreams. Our first call was to the Parish Church as we were part of a funeral procession but the cheerlessness of the occasion did not take from my sense of awe at the surroundings nor prevent me from attempting to comprehend this big experience in my life. As children we went to Mass in the small rural Church in Brickens but it paled almost to insignificance when I first laid my eyes on Saint Colman's. It would be an understatement to say that I was stunned by its size and beauty.

My brother's description of the town had done it less than justice. I have since visited every city in Ireland, some in Europe, The Middle East and The United States but none of these great sights left such an imprint on my mind as did my first view of Claremorris.

FIRST SIGHT OF AN AEROPLANE

We were in a hayfield where my father was shaking out freshly-cut grass when he shouted to me to look skyward at the aeroplane. I must have been about six or seven years old. It was difficult for me to accept that there were people within that noisy contrivance which appeared to be little bigger than a large bird. I remember his patience in trying to answer my many questions concerning how they got it up in the sky, and more importantly how would they come down. A couple of years later there was great excitement in our district as a result of the forced landing of a small plane on the lands of Charles Treston in nearby Cloontreston. Nobody was injured and the plane was only slightly damaged. Before being repaired and taken away several days later, crowds of sightseers came to inspect the rare novelty and it was big news in local newspapers and a topic of conversation in the district for many weeks. Incidentally it was more than fifty years after I saw an aeroplane for the first time before I boarded one, although my visits to Shannon, Dublin and Cork airports were frequent.

MY FIRST TELEPHONE CALL

I was sixteen years old when I first took a telephone receiver in my hand. My mother had suffered a fractured femur when she fell as she was dismounting from her bicycle outside Dunleavy's house. She was taken by ambulance to the County Hospital in Castlebar that night and my brother, John, travelled with her. He remained overnight in Castlebar and after her operation the next morning he contacted me by telephone to advise me of the outcome. I was an apprentice to the hardware business in Warde's of Claremorris but like ninety per cent of householders at that time they had no telephone, so he put the call through to Tierneys. Pat Tierney, who sent a messenger for me, then stood beside me as he showed me how to use the apparatus.

Despite my belated dêbut, in due course I spent six extremely happy years working as a telephone attendant in Claremorris head post office where I played a part in connecting thousands of telephone calls to places right across the world.

FIRST NIGHT IN A HOTEL

It was during my late teens that I first stayed overnight in a hotel. A business transaction required my presence in a distant town and the only train suitable to me arrived there in the late evening. Entering the hotel, I knocked at the reception desk, there being no bell, and a friendly, elderly man appeared and greeted me. He showed me to my room and queried the time at which I wished to be called on the following morning.

At the precise time there was a knock on my door and the same man's voice called out "Your shaving water, sir." There was hot water on tap in the bedrooms of few provincial hotels in those days and not many people had heard of electric razors. It is difficult to know whether it was embarrassed or important I felt on being titled "Sir" by a man three times my age but anyway it was another "first" in my life.

On opening the bedroom door to take in the hot water I saw pairs of highly polished gents' shoes outside other bedroom doors. It was part of hotel service everywhere for porters in the early hours each morning to polish all shoes left outside bedroom doors. This service continued up to the nineteen sixties and many tales have been told of pranks played by guests on their fellow guests by hiding shoes and switching them about.

CHRISTMAS

Whenever adults are asked to recall the most salient memories of childhood they will invariably include Christmas. As well as being a happy time it was exciting and full of expectancy.

For me it began with Advent when the teacher in our school got the younger pupils to promise that they would say one thousand Hail Marys over the coming four weeks in preparation for the Feast. Every few days she inquired from the pupils what progress they had made and it was a manifestation of the strength of faith of all concerned that there was never the slightest doubt that anybody might be cheating. We all had them said by Christmas.

It was the custom that the parents in every household went to the local town on the fowl market day. The father went in a cart drawn by either a horse or a donkey and the mother followed later on a bicycle. In the cart there was likely to be from fifteen to twenty turkeys or geese. Geese were bred and reared by farmers who had wet or low-lying land but while we had our share of this type of ground my parents preferred to rear turkeys. They claimed that geese soiled a large area where calves also grazed, while turkeys could be confined to a garden.

The fowl were sold at the market and the proceeds were used to buy "the Christmas." This would consist of a large box containing, in addition to the usual groceries, a variety of goods that would not be seen again until the following Christmas. There would be a three-gallon jar of porter and a bottle of whiskey. Also included would be tinned fruit, candied peel, loaf sugar and jams and marmalades packed in jugs which would be used later for containing milk or water. We still have one of these jugs which must be about sixty years old.

Also included in the big box but carefully concealed from the eyes of youngsters were toys and other little presents which in due course found their ways to the welcoming hands of children. A letter to Santa Claus was always a "must" and he never failed to pay his visit. On the night of Christmas Eve, stockings were hung on the crane at the open-hearth fireplace. He brought dolls to girls and small toys to boys, but he also brought useful articles like pencils, stockings and maybe a jumper. It amazed me how he always knew exactly what each of us needed and he never made the mistake of putting them in the wrong stocking. On one occasion when about to write to him I suggested to my mother that it would be wise to request at least a dozen pencils and a few pairs of shoes seeing that there was no charge. She quickly explained that there were many other children to get presents and he might very well decide to give nothing at all to anybody who was too greedy. I heeded her advice not to overdo the asking.

There was no Christmas tree in our house or in any neighbour's house. Our only decoration apart from about twenty Christmas cards which stood on the mantelpiece was a plentiful adornment of holly which was placed over every picture and statue. A few sprigs protruded from over the dishes on the dresser. We could afford to be lavish with this item because a wild holly tree grew on our bog where it still survives.

We had no miniature crib but its absence probably lent more meaning to our visits to the one in the Church.

The old custom of leaving a candle lighting in every window is now almost forgotten. Traditionally it signified a guide to Saint Joseph and The Blessed Virgin and a welcome for them in every house which was in direct contrast to the inn in Bethlehem where there was no room for them.

In every grocery shop "regular" customers were given a "Christmas box."A regular customer was one who called to purchase goods often throughout the year but not necessarily on a weekly or fortnightly basis. The size of the Christmas box depended on the amount of business the customer did in a shop and it could be large enough to include a bottle of whiskey, a Christmas cake, cigarettes or tobacco and a few items of grocery. A Christmas box was expected from every grocer, including the eggler or travelling shop, but it did not apply to the draper, butcher, chemist or hardware merchant.

Many a shopkeeper lost a customer by not giving a "decent" Christmas box while some cunning traders gave more than the customers were worth, knowing that it would be a topic of conversation in the rural areas, and in this way they hoped to lure new customers to their premises. Sometimes they succeeded.

On St. Stephen's Day we were always awakened early by the sound of mouth organ music played by wren boys who were dressed up in old tattered clothes and wearing false faces. They called to every house looking for money to bury the wren (pronounced "ran"). I never saw a dead wren but it was an old barbarous custom indulged in for centuries to hunt and kill a wren and then carry it from door to door. Thankfully this unwanted killing ceased many decades past but it is regrettable that the custom of youngsters going out in disguise playing their music and collecting the few pence has died out but in some areas there are signs of revival.

A factor that helped to make Christmas special in some homes was the arrival of parcels from America or letters containing dollars. Although I had a number of uncles and aunts in the States neither a parcel nor a dollar ever entered through our door. Of much greater social importance was the return of emigrants for the festive season. They brought colour and enjoyment to the whole neighbourhood as well as to their family homes.

RURAL WEDDINGS

I could have scarcely been more than three years old when Austin Ruane got married. Our houses were within fifty yards of each other and while each had its own separate entrance from the by-road there was a small iron gate in the centre of the mearing wall which rendered strolling in and out much easier. The humdrum of our everyday carefree lives was interrupted on that sunny day when the largest gathering of people that I ever saw, assembled in a convivial and happy atmosphere. It was in such contrast to our normal pattern that the memory has remained with me.

Austin's wedding to Delia Mary Mortimer from Murneen was typical of all rural weddings of the time. Although far from the glittering occasions of the present time they were nonetheless equally enjoyable. The groom, accompanied by the best man and two close friends one of whom traditionally was a married woman, not necessarily a relative, left the groom's home in the morning or early afternoon in a horse-drawn trap or sidecar and they travelled to the home of the bride. Other guests also travelled but in their own time. They spent some hours there mingling with the bride's family and relatives. At a prearranged time they left in separate vehicles for the Church in the bride's parish for the celebration of the marriage ceremony.

Immediately afterwards the newly married couple entered the groom's vehicle and they proceeded to his home where the wedding festivities were scheduled to take place. All the guests who were invited to the church followed them in close procession in their own traps and sidecars. This convoy was called a "drag." As they neared the groom's house bonfires comprising of straw and sticks were set alight and neighbours stood nearby cheering and waving their hands. On arrival the guests who had not been at the Church were waiting to greet the newly weds who entered the house to more hand-clapping and congratulations. On the rare occasions when the groom went to live in the bride's house the celebrations took place in her home. This arrangement was described as the groom "marrying in to the place."

Willing hands unyoked the horses and tethered them leaving them with a supply of hay. Then the revelling commenced with guests getting plenty of food and drink. This was followed by music and dancing right throughout the night usually ending the next morning when it was time to go home to milk the cows or get their children ready for school. The music was always supplied by unpaid local musicians.

No wedding was complete without a visit from a group of strawboys who were called "folpers." They were disguised in a somewhat similar manner to wrenboys. There were usually about six in the group. On entering the house they beckoned girls to partner them in a dance and the bride was always one of those so requested. Not a single word was spoken by them and after one dance they were offered drink which was never refused because indeed to get drink was partly the reason for their coming. They then politely took their departure to a round of applause.

Some guests had their own traps or sidecars but those who did not possess any transport got lifts from neighbours. Others still, especially relatives who had come long distances or who lived in the town, had to hire jarveys.

I do not remember jarveys plying for hire but my father hired one for his own wedding although he owned his own horse and sidecar. The jarvey was his cousin, John Higgins, who inherited his parents' small farm in Cloonfaughna. By this time he had sold the farm and with the proceeds purchased a house in Church Street, Claremorris where he started a very successful business as a jarvey. In due course the house was purchased by John Smyth who demolished it and built a substantial residence on the site. Significantly perhaps, he provided a modern version of the same type of service having had a hackney car for most of his life.

John Higgins had passed on before my time but I was well acquainted with his son, Michael Joe, who taught for many years in Cullane National

School. After moving to Moycullen he was elected to Galway County Council which gave him a forum to express openly his deeply held republican views as well as allowing him to use his talents as a distinguished public representative. One of his daughters was appointed a District Justice having the honour to be one of the first women ever to grace the bench.

I visited him when he was in the Mater Hospital some time before his death in the sixties. I was then a member of Mayo County Council and it was my sad duty a short time later to propose a motion of sympathy on his death when glowing tributes were paid by other members to his work as a teacher and as a great Irish nationalist.

WAKES AND FUNERALS

My uncle-in-law, Mike Fitzpatrick, died suddenly while harrowing soil in a field of conacre which he had rented from John Ruane in Caraun. John was walking beside him when Mike collapsed and died instantly from a massive heart attack. He had never been ill for even one day during his life so the shock was traumatic and the grief profound.

His remains were taken to his house where the wake was held. It was the first time that I had been at a wake or had seen a corpse. The whole scene was distressing as indeed is every occasion of sorrow. My aunt and her family cried inconsolably and they seemed to get worse with the arrival of new callers, many of whom were also crying. My parents brought my brother, Séamus, and myself home at around midnight.

We went back to my aunt's house the next morning and we remained there until the remains were removed to the Parish Church in Claremorris that evening. People continued to call right through the day and everybody was offered a drink. The funeral homes of modern times have largely dispensed with wakes but on the rare occasions when the old custom applies the scene has not changed.

Although it was in the very early thirties there were about twelve motor cars in the funeral one of them being a hackney car hired by my father. The remains were conveyed in a motor hearse but about fifteen years later horse-drawn hearses were still in service, in various places, including Ballyhaunis. Two big horses, discreetly adorned with black harness and with black plumes placed on their heads drew the vehicle while the driver, who, with the exception of a white shirt, was dressed entirely in black from his hard hat and long overcoat to his shining boots, sat on a high seat immediately behind the animals. The section within which the coffin was enclosed was but little different in design and decoration from the modern motor hearse of today.

Long after World War Two was over a horse-drawn hearse was used by an undertaker in Society Street in Ballinasloe. During that time a local hackney car proprietor in the same town had a small trailer-hearse which he attached to the towbar on his car. To me the concept was unique because I have never seen one anywhere else. It had an economic advantage for the mourners because they had to pay for only one vehicle to convey themselves and the remains to the Church and to the graveyard.

All female members of a bereaved family dressed entirely in black at the funeral and they continued to remain so attired for one year to signify a state of mourning. Some widows appeared in public only in black clothes for the remainder of their lives. The male members wore black ties for twelve months and some also wore small diamond-shaped pieces of crepe on the sleeves of their coats. All kinds of enjoyment and celebration like going to pictures, dances and weddings were forsaken for the year. The custom died out several years ago with few lamenting its passing. It was often hypocritical, being merely a ritual rather than an expression of genuine grief.

When told in school about funeral offerings we got the impression that they applied only in the dim and distant past – probably in the last century. But on attending a funeral in Westmeath in 1975 it surprised me to find that the practice was still in vogue there. As soon as the requiem Mass was over and before the remains were removed from the Church the chief mourner was joined by the celebrant, who was also the parish priest, as they stood at a small table placed beside the coffin. Members of the congregation then went up and placed money on the table. The money went entirely to church funds but it was an accepted fact that people paid not according to their means but in keeping with the esteem in which the deceased or the family were held. The presence of the mourner ensured the maximum response.

REFUSE DISPOSAL

Prior to the introduction of scavenging services householders in Claremorris had to dispose of their refuse in the local dump which was situated by the lake off the Brookhill road. Few people in the town owned suitable transport but they were well served in this regard by a local man who was known as "Soldier". How such a name was bestowed on him was unknown, but a more unlikely specimen of a warrior would be difficult to find. Even when cold sober, in his gait and in his speech he always gave the impression of being slightly inebriated, and while partial to a drop of the black stuff he was seldom under the influence. The scavenging service provided by him with his grey pony and cart was first class, and his charges were very reasonable.

"Soldier," who appeared to be ageless, lived in Cloonconnor, on a small farm, the produce of which he sporadically sold in the market. On one occasion, having failed to dispose of a load of straw by late evening, he requested everybody who passed by, young and old, male and female to purchase it. Having been totally ignored for a long time, it was a welcome relief to have an enquiry about the price from a young Ardroe schoolboy. "Soldier" asked for ten shillings and the young fellow, wishing to befool him, said his father would pay the money and accept the straw if it was delivered to him. Poor "Soldier" brought it to Ardroe which was a journey of almost a mile. He opened the gate of the private house and was about to tip the load when the owner appeared and asked him what he was doing. The man, who owned less than half a rood of a garden and did not possess even a dog, tried to explain that straw was of no use to him and that there must have been some error.

Now "Soldier" was normally a mild-mannered and inoffensive type of man who was not easily ruffled but this was too much for him. Seeing through the ruse he turned the pony around, but before taking his departure he used a diatribe of language about the man's son that could scarcely be described as parliamentary with such volume that he was heard a long distance away. Among those who heard him was the schoolboy who was on his way home, but he had enough sense to hide in a neighbouring house until "Soldier" was well on his way back to the market square. How he explained away the incident to his father is another story.

The introduction of a scavenging service by Mayo County Council in 1966 put an end to the need for Soldier's services in that area. Outside of those within the Urban District Councils, Claremorris was the first town in Mayo to get this service. As the dump was an eyesore and a health hazard in close proximity to the town, its closure some years ago was welcomed by everybody, except by those who lived nearer to the new location which in turn is now set to close.

"Soldier" departed this life many years ago and his demise left Claremorris bereft of one of its most unique characters.

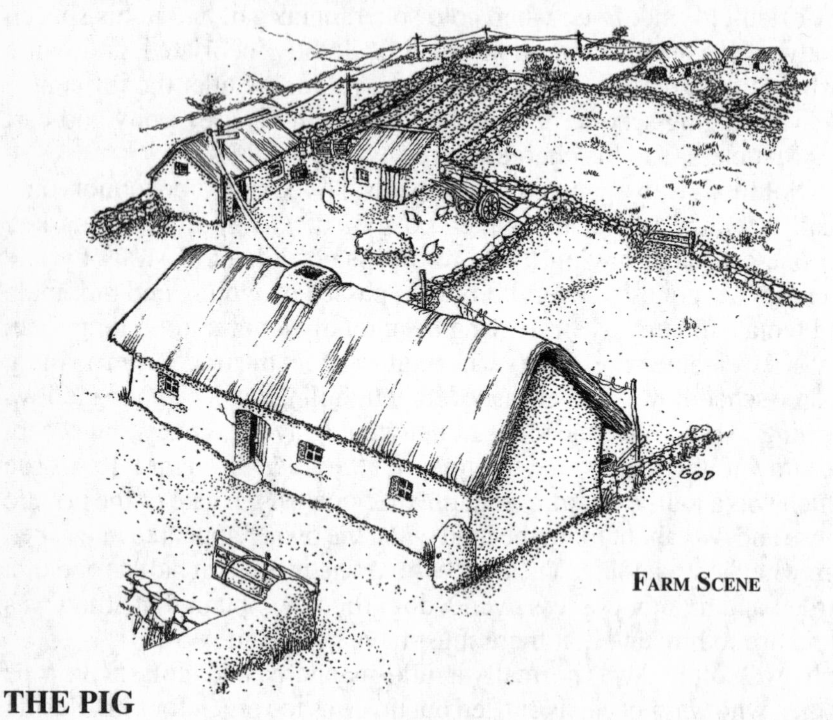

FARM SCENE

THE PIG

The pig, which has disappeared from the rural scene, was very much a part of a farmyard, and in every townland a few farmers each kept a sow, as we did ourselves. This prolific animal produced two litters of bonhams or piglets per year and the number in each litter varied from ten to sixteen.

As farrowing time took several hours the little bonhams were taken away from their mother as soon as they were born and shortly after the last arrival they were placed in lines one by one to suckle on the sow's two rows of teats while she lay on her side. A sow had either twelve or fourteen teats and if she had more bonhams than teats the surplus was given to some neighbour who reared them by bottle feeding for the first few weeks until they were able to consume swill. After a bonham had the first suckle it recognised that teat as its own and thenceforth it would not suckle from any other. It was nature's way of ensuring that when the sow lay down to feed them there was no fighting among them. The teats nearest to the front produced more and better milk and the farmer always put the weaker bonhams on these. That of course kept the stronger ones to the rear and the idea was to keep a balance on the progress of the litter as a whole.

When the bonhams were about nine weeks old they were weaned and with the exception of two or three they were taken to the market. They were sold usually in pairs or in threes to other farmers who then fed them on potatoes, cabbage, mangolds, turnips, meal and milk for a further number of weeks until they were mature enough to be slaughtered. The sow owner did likewise with those he kept over. Each year one was kept for killing for the household use and in a district where there was a bacon factory the remainder were brought there by cart while in other places they were taken to fairs where they were purchased by pig dealers on behalf of the factories.

Killing a pig on the farm was a major operation. The animal was kept fasting from the previous day and in the morning he was led to his doom where a butcher's knife and a scaffold consisting of the kitchen table awaited him. The gory details I will omit.

After the killing the intestines were removed and the carcass, having been attached to a ladder, was left hanging upright overnight. The intestines were cleaned, boiled, turned inside out and cleaned and boiled again. They were then filled with a mixture of blood which was saved at the killing, oatmeal, onions and spices of various kinds. They were tied at the top and boiled for a considerable time and when taken out of the water they were real black puddings which for flavour, richness and taste could not be equalled by any factory production.

On the following day the carcass was taken down and boned and the meat was placed in layers in a barrel or a box. The bottom was covered with coarse salt up to a depth of three inches and a coating of similar thickness was placed between each layer. In this way the bacon was cured. It was taken out as required by the housewife and after a time lapse some people took out large pieces of the bacon which they hung from crooks in the ceiling. They believed that it cured better outside of the box, but it was surely less hygienic.

The ribs and shanks were not salted but along with the newly made black puddings they were presented in small amounts to neighbours.

Only a similar small quantity was kept for the family because being fresh it would not remain in an edible state for many days. In the weeks following as neighbours killed their own pigs they too distributed these portions in a similar way so that for the early weeks of Winter there was fresh pork and black pudding in most rural houses.

A great social occasion was the cardplaying for the pig's head. A group of nine neighbouring men (and it was always men) sat around the kitchen table playing "25." There were others present, including women and children, but as nine was the maximum that could play at one sitting they played "25" at another table for a few pennies or else they stayed by the fire chatting until somebody won the head. Afterwards it was tea and currant cake for everybody and the usual talk and laughter so typical of country house visiting.

DOGS AND THEIR USES

No farmhouse was without at least one dog. Rover, Captain, Shepherd, Bran, Sailor, and Daisy were common names for dogs but if one possessed a distinguishing mark or colour he might be called Spot, Darkie or Snowy. When his name was called out by any member of the household a dog always responded by running immediately to the caller.

My father was somewhat original in putting the name Sergeant on one of our dogs. Like most farmers he was quite expert in training them to do his bidding. But while most were happy to get them to round up cattle and sheep he went further by teaching them simple tricks. He taught them to roll over on the floor when told to do so, and to stand upright on their hind legs and beg for food. He also got them to ask for food by giving one loud, clear bark. But his most entertaining trick was to get them to run into a corner pretending to be terrified when he would say "Hide, the guards are coming and your licence is unpaid." A guard called annually to every house to take the census and while he was filling the forms in our house my father always got the dog to perform the trick. It was an unfailing source of amusement.

A TALE MY FATHER TOLD ME

A man from the next townland to Garryedmond who was well known to my father emigrated to England at the beginning of the twentieth century when he was about twenty years of age. Of good appearance and physique and conventional in every way he kept in regular touch with his parents and family by letter. Unmarried, a strict teetotaller and a willing worker, his only form of relaxation was a holiday at his parents' home.

About ten years after leaving home for the first time, he arrived back for his usual bi-annual holiday. The passenger train taking him from Dublin was delayed and when alighting from it in Claremorris it was well after midnight. The era of the taxi was still in the future and jarveys did not ply for hire from the railway station at night, so there was no alternative to picking up his suitcase and setting out on foot for his parents' home. It was a moonlight night and the distance was little more than two miles.

Shortly after turning off the main road at Drimneen he observed a group of people walking slowly ahead of him, and while catching up with them the light from the moon became so bright that it was almost like daylight. Those at the rear he recognised and then, peering through the crowd, he spotted many familiar faces. But there was something both tense and eerie about the whole scenario which he could not pinpoint.

He greeted those nearest to him and asked where they were going. They did not even look at him but completely ignored his question as well as his greeting, while they continued to talk among themselves about the virtues of a certain man.

Slowly it dawned on him that the man they were discussing was dead and that he himself was marching in a funeral procession. Listening closely he was disconcerted to learn that they were talking about a neighbour who had died twelve years earlier. What made the scene both familiar and frightening was the fact that he was now walking in a ghostly re-enactment of a funeral which he had attended before emigrating for the first time.

The scene appeared totally real except for the fact that everybody present cold-shouldered him. Looking through the crowd he clearly remembered that the same people were present twelve years previously but some had died in the meantime. Seeing himself in the position he had occupied in the actual funeral and still wearing the same outdated clothes caused him to fear that he was the ghost, so pinching himself and discovering feeling made it reasonable to assume that he was still alive.

The cortêge continued towards Ballinasmalla graveyard which was only a couple of hundred yards away. The gate was open and the mourners entered following the coffin which was carried by the deceased's two sons and two neighbours.

He stood on the road for a few moments until they went out of his sight. Adding to his distress, the moonlight then dimmed, and scarcely able to walk due to fright, he continued on his way. Fearing that he would be unable to make it to his parents' home which was only a short distance away, he knocked on the door of a roadside house. Although they were in bed, the occupants rose to admit him and in a state of near collapse he told his incredible tale.

They knew that he was genuinely frightened because he was a solid, sensible man who was cold sober and never given to fantasies, pranks or funny stories. They were satisfied that he truly believed he had seen an apparition which was not of this world. They made tea and kept him until later in the morning when the man of the house accompanied him to his parents' home.

He remained at home for a few weeks before returning to England and during that time the experience did not appear to have had any ill-effect on him.

Was it real or was it hallucination? Nobody can tell, but what can be told for certain is that so convinced was the man of having seen something supernatural which had a message for him, the meaning of which he could not fathom, that a short time later he entered a monastery and became a lay brother. No unusual manifestation was ever again experienced by him and he lived a devout, prayerful and happy life until his death at a ripe old age. He is buried in the monastery grounds. Some of his relatives still live in Claremorris district.

GARRYEDMOND FORGE

Although the blacksmith cum farrier had ceased working by the time I started walking to Mass in Brickens the forge in Garryedmond was still standing at the road junction for Cloontooa. It was a wooden structure with a corrugated iron roof and after the departure of the blacksmith it was used as a cattle shed. Nearby were the ruins of its predecessor, the old stone built forge and the dwelling house to which it was attached. These ruins were visible until recent times.

The last blacksmith to live in the old stone house was named Cussane and he eventually emigrated with his wife and family. After a time the roof fell in. Some years later another blacksmith named Tom Flynn arrived with his wife and family in the townland and they rented the house left vacant by the Tullys who had emigrated. Tom expressed an interest in opening a farrier business but he had no forge. The neighbours got together and from their own resources they purchased the building materials for a new structure. It was erected by voluntary labour close to the old one on a site donated by Jim Dunleavy. The new blacksmith worked there for some years but whatever the reason, he left the area, and the forge was closed down never to be reopened.

The Flynn family became close friends of my parents and I particularly recall the many visits to our house of Tom's teenaged daughter, Peggy, during my very early childhood. Many years after their departure the news of her untimely death in extremely tragic circumstances reached Garryedmond bringing deep shock and sorrow to those who remembered her.

There was great affection and respect for the blacksmith in rural Ireland. Every forge was a meeting place where men congregated to discuss local events or affairs of State while the blacksmith continued with his work as he savoured their deliberations. His job required such skill that no "gobán" could emulate it. A handyman could build a wall, nail together a wooden gate, sew a button or give a haircut to a neighbour, but only a blacksmith had the ability or the facility to shoe a horse or a donkey, make a tongs or do any other work with iron or steel. Always to the forefront in patriotism they have secured an honoured place in Irish history and folklore because they made the pikes for the rebels in their many encounters with the invaders down through the years. They will be remembered forever for the part they played in the 1798 rebellion, especially in County Wexford.

The new forge cum cattle shed has long since disappeared from Garryedmond but the junction is still known locally as "the forge." For many years it was the venue for the bonfire on the eve of St. John's Day when huge crowds gathered from as far away as Loughanemon, Carrowbeg, Rannaghard and Brickens.

THE BELLMAN OR TOWN CRIER

Except on pig-fair mornings and on the weekly market day, there was very little noise on the streets of Ballyhaunis during the forties. Apart from the daily Westport/Longford bus which rolled through the town each morning and returned nightly, and the odd petrol tanker and haulage lorry passing through, the most common disturbances were the occasional barking of dogs and the chatter of children on their way home from school.

But one different and indeed unique sound was sometimes literally ringing in our ears. It was generated by Martin Deignan, the bellman, doing his rounds. For a small fee he advertised everything and anything of local interest. It could be a dance in McGarry's Hall, a concert, a play or a card drive in the parochial hall, a sale by a local auctioneer, the coming of a circus or a meeting in the Central Hotel of a trade union branch, dramatic society or the local boxing club.

His circuit commenced at the top of Upper Main Street when six or seven loud peals of his handbell eclipsed all other sounds. Slowly he walked in the centre of the streets which were invariably traffic-free in wartime Ireland and the stronger and more rapidly he swung the bell, the louder was the clang of the clapper striking the hollow metal. When he stopped ringing, the fading of the chime into the still evening air was his cue to start speaking. The first two words of every message were delivered at the top of his voice and they never varied. "Don't forget !", he bellowed, and this appeared to be a complete sentence. After a few seconds of a pause he continued with the announcement in a tone pitched much lower, but still audible at a considerable distance.

A typical bulletin would be: "Don't forget to-morrow night in McGarry's Hall, Ballyhaunis Draughts Club hold their annual dance. Music by Stephen Garvey and admission five shillings." He believed in using only as many words as were necessary, and he repeated the procedure every fifty or sixty yards until the whole town was enlightened about the upcoming event.

If given a few shillings extra, or if he liked the organisers, the message might be delivered more often on the route and perhaps a few extra steps would be taken beyond the town perimeter. He seldom found it necessary to use notes as the announcements were generally short and he was familiar with every local organisation, activity and venue.

All conversation in the pubs and shops ceased momentarily when the sound of the bell drew close, and people listened to see if the message held any interest for themselves. In a case of urgency the bellman gave an invaluable service and it was often supplemental to advertising in local newspapers.

Martin Deignan, who was also the local billposter, was well known to the publicity managers of circuses and travelling shows, all of whom availed of his services. He usually referred to himself as "the principal billposter in this town." Nobody could dispute his claim because he was the only one.

3

Going to School

KOILMORE NATIONAL SCHOOL

The school building was situated in Koilmore about one mile from my home, and according to a plaque high on the outside front wall it was erected in 1893. Falling numbers resulted in its closure in the early seventies and when sold some time later, the new owners demolished it. Memories for most of us who passed through it would be mixed, but I think we all would concede that despite many imperfections it gave us a good grounding and served us well as we made our way in the world later.

Although little more than four years old at the time, my recollection of my first day in school is very clear. It was a far cry from the kindergarten schools of today. At that tender age it was with grave trepidation that I left home in the morning with my brother Séamus who was almost two years older, taking me by the hand. A neighbouring boy, Martin James Concannon, who was a couple of years older still, called for us as he had called every morning since Séamus commenced going to school. He later went to England where he settled down many years ago but our friendship continued. The cause of the fear was due in no small measure to a question which my mother had asked Séamus every evening when he came home from school and it was a question which every other mother also asked her offspring: "Did you get any slap today?"

I was put seated at a desk and although a few of the pupils were known to me, there was no nicety such as putting me sitting beside someone with whom I was acquainted. It was a mixed school with two teachers: The principal was James Murphy who taught third to seventh classes inclusive in the large room, while the assistant teacher who was

KOILMORE SCHOOL

his wife, taught low and high infants, first and second classes in a smaller room. There was a third class-room which was vacant for many years as far as pupils were concerned but it was used for storing turf. Early on the first morning a little girl was told by the teacher to distribute plasticine among the infants. She left some in front of me and never having seen the likes before I assumed that it was for eating. I was in the act of putting it into my mouth when the child beside me whispered that it was not meant to be eaten but to be used for making into shapes of various kinds. Along with the plasticine incident my abiding memories of that first day in school are of seeing other children crying after being slapped with a rod, and the deep sorrow I felt for them as well as the terror I endured at the whole set up.

JOHN BOLAND'S DIRECTIVE

It is difficult to believe that it is only a few short years since John Boland, God bless him, as Minister for Education abolished the barbaric practice of beating children in schools. He encountered much opposition from various groups throughout the community at the time, and indeed he is still criticised by some for not first arranging alternative disciplinary measures to replace it. There can be no denying the fact that discipline is necessary but as nobody has submitted an acceptable working alternative for well over a hundred years, it is obvious that were we to wait for such, there are thousands of children in our country today who are reasonably happy who would still be getting their daily dose of beating at the whim of teachers.

As in every other walk of life there were teachers who were totally unsuited to the profession either because of temperament or inability to teach, while of course others were compassionate, reasonable and a credit to their calling. However there was no teacher who did not have a cane, sally rod or strap on the desk, and until John Boland's directive no single child escaped physical punishment.

THE MASTER'S ROOM

My first four years there must have been quite uneventful because I remember little about them except that I moved up a class each year. Entering third class on my fifth year also meant changing to the bigger classroom and from then on having "The Master" as teacher. Although every day embodied a measure of fear there were also some relaxing moments. Caretakers were unheard of in any rural school and the older and stronger boys always rushed for the sweeping brushes each morning before classes commenced. One of them sprinkled water on the floor while two or three others swept up the dust and dirt. In the Winter other boys put sods of turf in the open grate after which they lit the fire. They also put the ashes of the previous day's fires in a bucket and this they dumped in a corner of the school yard. In the meantime two or three girls got dusters and they went through the routine of dusting whether or not there was any dust about.

Nobody was ever told to do those jobs. There was no need because they just continued to do what generations of children before them had done and they were chores that everybody wanted to do. It was not that they loved cleanliness but the operations could take up to fifteen minutes during which time the teachers were relaxing. The more time that could be wasted the longer the terror of the day was postponed, and every extra minute counted.

After the cleaning, and with brushes and dusters back in their places the roll was called and then it was down to business for the day.

It was extraordinary how one teacher could teach five classes at the same time and in the one room. Sometimes he grouped third and fourth and had them doing arithmetic for example, and he might group fifth and sixth for history and leave seventh at geography. On another occasion he might put fourth and fifth studying a subject, and deal similarly with sixth and seventh while leaving third on their own, but often each class was working on a subject on its own. Admittedly the number of pupils was small and the average in Koilmore school in my time would be about fifty.

An Inspector called occasionally. We had a few examinations but on most of his visits he only checked the roll book and talked privately to the teacher for about an hour.

THE CATECHISM EXAMINATION

All the priests of the parish visited the schools regularly. They seldom examined us on religious affairs but gave little talks or lectures. There was a religious examination once a year and for a month beforehand we were studying catechism day after day to the exclusion of almost all other subjects. The Diocesan Examiner came on the appointed day and he meticulously examined each class in the school in great detail. The tension was almost unbearable when a pupil was unable to answer a question correctly. In those times nearly every subject, and especially catechism, had to be learned off by heart, but the meaning of much of it was beyond our comprehension. If the overall result of the examination was reasonably good we all relaxed, and if finished an hour or so before normal school closing time of 3 p.m. we got the remainder of the day off. On the other hand if the result was disappointing the remainder of the day was devoted to another examination by the teacher and a good caning for every question missed. After that day religious study was largely put on the back burner until a month before the following year's examination.

RAMBLES IN ÉIRINN

If James Murphy was hard on the pupils he was equally hard on himself, and he taught to the best of his ability. In his favour it must also be said that there were no favourites and everybody got the same treatment. He was a true Irishman with a heart animated by love of his country who beyond question inspired patriotism into every pupil who passed through his school. Our poetry was always of the nationalistic and well nigh rebel variety, mainly that of Thomas Davis, many of whose poems I can still recite by heart.

His favourite English Reader was *Rambles in Éirinn* by William Bulfin. As a very young man, the author, who was a native of the midlands, emigrated to South America where he became a journalist with *The Southern Cross*. After his appointment to the editorship of that newspaper he returned to Ireland to combine a cycling tour of the country with a holiday. Afterwards he described the expedition in a series of articles and these were later compounded into a book with the title *Rambles in Éirinn.*

As Bulfin travelled through the country each district reminded him of famous people or battles associated with it. We accompanied him in spirit to scenes of romance and tragedy as he recalled deeds of bravery and of treachery. He sketched almost every legendary, literary, military, political and religious name of note in Irish history, from Fionn MacCumhaill to those of his own day and his analysis included the bad as well as the good – the traitor along with the patriot.

Bulfin revelled in the natural, unspoiled beauty which he saw almost everywhere in Ireland, and his writings passionately expressed his perceptions. *Rambles in Éirinn* taught us more about Irish history than did our history books, and more about the geography of Ireland than the atlas.

SINGING, SEWING AND SERVING

We had singing classes of half an hour each on two evenings per week, but I was not blessed with a singing voice. However, I can still remember the words of songs most of which were in Irish. Some of my classmates will, I feel sure, recall *Seán O'Duibhir an Ghleanna, Bán Chnoic Éireann Ó, Anois'teacht an Earraigh* and *Fir an Iarthair.* At the beginning of this century the English version of the last named (*The Men of the West,* by William Rooney) was translated into Irish by Dr. Conor Maguire of Claremorris who was Dr. Roderick Maguire's grandfather.

Each Friday evening all the girls went into Mrs. Murphy's room for sewing and knitting classes. Meanwhile the boys learned in Latin *The manner of serving a priest at Mass.* At that time Mass was said entirely in Latin and although no boy from our school was ever asked to serve we still had to learn the formula. Except in very few instances Mass is said nowadays only in the vernacular and girls serve as well as boys.

MY CLASS

The class to which I belonged was the largest in the school having about ten pupils. There were five long desks in the Master's room facing his table and partly to his right as he faced us. Four smaller desks along by the front wall faced diagonally across to the centre of the room. We usually sat in the centre desks. No place was reserved for any pupil but usually seated on my left was John Donnelly from Ballinagran, who in due course inherited his family farm where he married and raised a family. On my right was Billy Waldron from Cartownacross. He went on to become a priest and for over forty years has ministered successfully in America. To this day I have carefully kept the souvenir card of his ordination on June 18th 1950.

We made our own ink by putting a quantity of water into a glass container and then adding a black powder until it reached the required strength. The china or delph inkwells on the desks were filled as required.

As the school playground was very small and was wet and muddy some of the time, we were allowed to play on the main road which ran by the front of the school building. We played the usual games like having a race, tig, and ball throwing. There were not many cars on the roads in those days and when the odd one approached we stood aside and let it pass. Boys and girls never mixed with each other during playtime.

THE PHOTOGRAPHER AND OTHER CALLERS

A photographer named Michael Flanagan from nearby Logboy called a few times over the years. His first call would be to the teacher with whom he would arrange to take photographs of the whole school at a later date, as well as individual ones for those who required them. So we would all be dressed in our Sunday clothes for the big occasion.

The actual taking of the photographs was a slow and cumbersome process. After organising the children in lines the photographer told them to keep still. He then set up his camera on a tripod. Having taken off his hat he pulled over his head a long black hood which was attached to the camera. The purpose of the hood was to keep out the light while he was looking through the lens to ensure that the picture was straight and that everybody was included. When everything was in order he clicked the lever which took the photograph.

It was seldom possible to get a group of small children to do what they were told, and again and again at least one turned away or moved about. Then the black hood had to be withdrawn from his head while they were reorganised and eventually he succeeded in getting a picture. A commercial traveller arrived with copies, pencils, pens, blotting paper and rubbers about once each quarter. The teacher always got supplies from him and we in turn bought those items as we required them.

The only means of heating was from the turf fire which was expected to keep the large draughty classroom warm. The turf was supplied by the parents, and one cart load was required from each family during the Winter. They tipped it at the gate and during playtime that day the boys had to carry it in their arms into the otherwise empty classroom and stack it tidily there. Nobody complained –rather we looked forward to it because we never succeeded in completing the task within the allotted time. Whatever additional period it took was regarded as a bonus in so far as we were away from the chores of school work.

WALKING TO SCHOOL

We walked over the sand road from my home until within three hundred yards of the school we entered the tarred road. Approaching the building from either side and about one hundred yards from it was an advance school sign of a red torch on a white background. Beneath the torch, which was the recognised emblem of learning, were the bilingual words "Scoil" and "School."

There were three points along the road which flooded to a depth of ten or twelve inches after heavy rain and we had to cross over the fences in order to avoid getting our shoes and feet wet. In due course most wore wellingtons in Winter while in Summer we went barefooted. On one occasion, just after crossing the railway line the flood was particularly deep, and walking through it even with wellingtons was not possible. Because of the wire fencing on the boundary of the railway property, and the depth of the drains on the other side, we could not cross. So all the pupils from Garryedmond, Cloontooa, Knockatubber and Cartownacross had to return home.

At that time the sand roads were maintained by contractors who, on a yearly basis, successfully tendered to the County Council for the contracts. It was our hard luck that the contractor for this particular road was Jim Goggins from Cartownacross. He was a man of great integrity who performed his work to the highest standard. Within a few hours of our returning home he had deepened the drain inside in the field thereby releasing the water. However when returning from school a few days later somebody got the bright idea of plugging the gullet. It took hard work carrying stones and scraws but we did a neat job and we were not detected. When the next spell of heavy rain came there was an artificially arranged flood but sadly for us it came on a Saturday. Jim Goggins was there immediately and when he discovered what we had been up to, he made the culverts so deep and so wide that it was impossible for mere children to plug them again with their bare hands.

THE STATION

Just beyond the railway line there was a double bend on an otherwise straight stretch of half a mile of the road. This bend was called "the station", because it was a halting point for those who reached it first each morning. The idea was that we all walked together from there, and if anybody was a little late, all were late. The bend gave the advantage to the early arrivals of being able to watch the teachers' car pass on the main road while they themselves could not be seen. The teachers always came about twenty minutes early in their 14.9 Ford, which bore the registered number IZ-295, so if we were all at the Station when it passed there was plenty of time to reach the school by 9.30 a.m. Of course the number plate could not be seen at that distance but scarcely any other car ever passed around that time in the mornings, and the teachers' car was easily distinguishable by its unusual beige colour with black roof.

The station was a facility which was not available to the children from Ballygowan, Ballykinave or Ballyglass because the teachers passed them on the road each morning. They sometimes dallied, because nobody wanted to be in school too early and loitering, like every misdemeanour, was a crime deserving of corporal punishment.

ON OUR WAY HOME

On our way home we crossed the railway again of course. Trains passed from Dublin to Westport and vice versa several times each day

Waiting for the Train to Pass

with unfailing regularity. Farmers did not carry watches and few indeed possessed them, because they were not really necessary. No matter how far some of their land or bog was from their houses they could see or hear the trains and everybody knew exactly which train had gone by and which one was due next. A passenger train went outwards from Claremorris at 8 a.m. and a goods train went inwards at 9. There was a goods out at 10.a.m. and a passenger inwards at 11.30 and so it went throughout the whole day. Men working in the fields or in the bog went home for the dinner when the 1 p.m. passenger train passed and to their evening meal after the 6.30 goods.

Our school closed at 3 p.m. each evening and a goods train went by at 3.30. It often took us the half hour to stroll the half mile from the school to the railway. Some of us occasionally stole large wire nails from our fathers' tool boxes in order to place them on the rails as a train approached. As the wheels of the engine went over them they were totally flattened and they then flew either under the train or out on the slope. Many were lost but those retrieved we kept as keepsakes often using them as knives and some we gave to boys who lived quite a distance from the railway and therefore did not have the opportunity of being able to manufacture such unique objects.

Despite the hazards of playing on the public road, carrying in turf, bringing water from the well, crossing the railway and crossing fences when the road was flooded there was never even a minor accident.

Close to the railway there was a cluster of four houses. The first was owned by Peter Foy who was a bachelor and a quiet spoken and refined gentleman. A young man named Ned Elwood was employed by him as a workman and he lived with him for some years until the beet factory opened in Tuam. Ned got a job in the new factory and I never heard of him again. There was a thick blackthorn hedge near Foy's house which yielded an abundance of sloes when in season. On many occasions we entered his garden to pick and eat these horribly sour fruits and we trampled his grass and sometimes damaged the loose stone wall and although he saw us regularly he never complained. When we had gone home he just repaired the knocked down wall.

One evening, when I was about seven or eight years old, he was whitewashing his house as we passed on our way home. Some mischief activated within me, and lifting a handful of mud from the roadside I successfully targetted his handiwork. Expecting him to chase me I prepared to run, but he just looked at me and smiled. Then taking a bucket of water he washed down the mud, after which he applied another coat of whitewash. Had he pursued me as I had expected and given me a clip in the ear as was warranted, the whole episode would have left my mind within a few days. But due to his reaction the memory remained and his tact was not lost on his young observers for he was not teased again.

GOOD BYE TO KOILMORE SCHOOL

When I was eleven years old my brother Séamus and I left Koilmore school and we went to Meelickmore which is one and a half miles further away. The sole reason was that our older brother, who had qualified about two years earlier, was appointed principal there. Even at that time there was anxiety in small two-teacher schools to keep up the average number of pupils, because if it went below a certain level it could be reduced to a one teacher school. This would result in the assistant becoming redundant and she would have no redress. In a similar situation today she would be placed on a panel and assured of another teaching post elsewhere, but there was no such provision in those days. Apart from helping with the numbers it seemed only natural in the circumstances for us go to Meelickmore, when my brother was teaching there.

BROWNE'S FLAG

About half a mile from Ballygowan bridge on our way to Meelickmore we passed by a commemorative grey stone by the roadside marking the spot where The Honourable Henry George Monck Browne – a member of the Browne family from Castlemacgarrett was accidentally shot dead many years previously. It appears that while out fowling one morning he tripped while crossing the fence and his loaded shotgun triggered accidentally, killing him instantly. Described locally as "Browne's Flag" and providing a landmark for many decades, it has now become so weather-beaten as to be unnoticeable by a stranger.

POST PRIMARY EDUCATION

There was an excellent secondary school for girls at the Convent of Mercy in Claremorris but none for boys nearer than Ballinrobe which was seventeen miles from my home. The only supplements to primary education available to boys in our locality were the commercial and Irish classes which were held for a few hours twice per week in the old town hall.

It was my great regret that St. Colman's College was not established until after my time. People who did not, until then, have ease of access to secondary schools, and who wished to increase their knowledge, had to depend on correspondence courses until vocational schools and third level institutions came to the rescue with night classes. In 1992, "Age Action Ireland" was established in Dublin and one of its primary aims was to further extra-mural education among our country's aging population. The tremendous success it has achieved to date speaks for itself. Under its aegis branches of the "University of the Third Age" have been established in a number of centres in Ireland including Galway. The U3A, as it has come to be known, is a university in the original sense of the word – a collective of mature persons devoted to learning. It is a co-operative of people who have finished their main parenting or full time employment responsibilities and are prepared to share educational, creative, social and recreational activities.

Members share their knowledge and experience, and develop their own capabilities by learning from one another, and they liaise with educational and other relevent organisations. There is no examination and neither degree, diploma nor certificate is awarded.

The first U3A was formed in Toulouse University in 1972 when the university provided access to its facilities and lectures to older people interested in continuing their learning activities. The idea was so successful that the movement spread rapidly and is now established in countries on the five continents. It has a worldwide Federation, and an annual international meeting is held in a different country each year. We now appear to be on the verge of emulating American society where countless numbers of their citizens continue to study throughout their lives. The launching in 1996 of the "Irish National Conference for the European Year of Lifelong Learning" was a positive step forward in bringing educational benefit to people of my generation who failed to secure secondary school accommodation on completing the national school curriculum.

4

Music and Dancing

REPLACING THE COUNTRY HOUSE DANCE

Over a period of ten to fifteen years, and while I was still in primary school, the dance hall gradually replaced the cinema as the main source of night entertainment for youth. The cinema, of course, catered for people of all age groups. So far as rural Ireland was concerned the dance hall was fast replacing the traditional country house dances which had regaled generations through the long Winter nights.

The farmhouse was ideal for such gatherings, as each had a large kitchen with a concrete floor. I have often seen sparks rising from a floor as the heel tips or protector studs of men's boots connected with it as they swung with their partners while set dancing. Farmhouses were generally built a reasonable distance away from the nearest neighbours. The reason was to ensure that each had a measure of privacy, and it also helped to minimise the problem of trespass by domestic fowl, which every farmer's wife had in abundance. This was a great advantage when dances or parties were held because the sound of music or revelry would not interfere with neighbours especially if they happened to be old or ill. Indeed dances would not be held in any locality where such existed except for a wedding celebration or on the night of a Stations.

Included in the list of dances held in country houses was The Set or Half Set, Barn Dance, Polka, Highland Fling, Siege of Ennis, and Old Time Waltz. The Foxtrot or Quick Step, and all forms of slow dancing were products of the dance hall age.

THE DANCING MASTER

Prior to the nineteen twenties, what we would today call dancing classes were held in farmhouses during the Winter nights. During this season a journeyman teacher-cum-musician known as a Dancing Master visited most townlands. Year after year he stayed in the same house, where he was eagerly awaited, and where he had full accommodation free of charge. In return he taught dancing to members of the household without accepting any fee, and for a small contribution he taught all comers. Hence most young people were highly skilled in set dancing and in many steps of reels, jigs and hornpipes. He stayed in the house for as long as his services were required, normally about two to three weeks, after which he moved to another house in the next or the second next townland. Those dancing masters were almost always bachelors, so they were in no hurry to leave an area. As well as welcome, there was great respect for them because they were better educated than their students or their hosts, and they always conducted themselves with dignity and professionalism.

In Garryedmond, the rendezvous for the Dancing Master was our house. Hence my father was a very good step dancer as were many of his peers. While he often spoke about him, the Dancing Master's name was never mentioned and it is possible that little was known about him beyond the fact that he taught dancing. My interest in him at that time was slight, and discussion on him only took place when my father was trying to teach me some of the steps which he himself had learned.To my regret I never mastered the art.

The music at the country house dances was unfailingly supplied by local musicians. The violin, or the fiddle as it was always called at that time, was the most popular of musical instruments. It was sometimes supplemented by melodeon, concertina or tin whistle. The Fitzpatrick brothers John and Jim from Garryedmond were excellent fiddlers, and such was the demand for their music that they played in houses as far away as ten miles. Like the other musicians of their day, they gave their services free of charge. Their only reward was the enjoyment they got from entertaining their friends and acquaintances who were less talented than themselves.

One house that was constantly available for dances was Stauntons of Cloontooa. It was occupied by an old lady and her two sons, Roger and Owen. As it was a visiting house a few people were liable to call any night. If two or more of each sex were there, Roger automatically took down the fiddle and a dance until the early hours ensued.

DANCE HALLS

The dance halls eventually put an end to country house dances. Before they could open for public dancing, a licence fee had to be paid. There were no conditions attached regarding the maximum numbers to be admitted; no fire regulations nor inspections by fire officers and no limit to admission charges. From the authorities point of view, the more patrons and the higher the charge the better, because there was an entertainment tax payable which was about twenty five per cent of the entrance fee. The tax was collected by sticking stamps on the back of tickets, which by law had to be handed individually to patrons as the entrance charges at the box office were paid. On entering the hall proper, the ticket was taken by a steward who tore it in half. He kept one half, and returned the other to the patron who was legally bound to hold on to it until the dance was over because it enabled Inspectors from the Revenue Commissioners to carry out checks. Inspectors made random visits to various halls where they made a head count of those present, and if the proprietor or dance organiser did not have a corresponding number of half tickets with torn stamps, he was in trouble because of obvious cheating. It cannot be denied that much cheating was done, especially when dances were run by local communities for fund raising. Patrons gladly paid the admission fee, got no tickets and if questioned were prepared to say that no money was paid because of some service they had given to the committee.

Most dance hall proprietors were generous with people who carried a number of passengers in their cars and they usually admitted the drivers free of charge. Of course when dance halls first appeared there were very few motor cars and it was not unusual for patrons to cycle up to twelve miles to dances. My own first introduction to a dance hall happened by chance one Summer Sunday evening when I was about sixteen years old. While cycling leisurely along by Spaddagh, a neighbouring chap named Jimmy Dunleavy, who was about three years my senior, arrived from the opposite direction. His suggestion that we would go to Bange's Hall in Larganboy seemed a good idea, and on the spur of the moment we set off. On the way I became a bit concerned about what my parents would say next day, but Jimmy was very reassuring. Anyway, as it happened, they only laughed at the whole escapade. Larganboy was about nine miles away, and night had fallen long before we reached it. We had no lights on our bicycles but that did not worry us. Few people could afford bicycle lamps at the time, and the only concern cyclists had in that regard was the possibility of meeting a garda which would ensure a summons to the next District Court. A large percentage of District Court business in those years were charges for cycling without lights and/or having unlicensed dogs. Irish society has changed much in the meantime. Bicycles were left as near as possible to the hall, lying against a wall or a fence alongside a couple of hundred others. If one did happen to have a lamp it was left on the bicycle together with a pump, and, if the weather was dry, a coat on the carrier. Locking a bicycle was unheard of, and yet on return it was sure to be there, exactly as it was left a few hours earlier.

DANCE BANDS

The music on that, my first night in Bange's Hall, was supplied by a six piece band, the proprietor and leader of which was one John Francis Finn, better known as John Fra. Standing centre stage, he himself played the violin with such gusto that the modern rock bands could learn much from him. He did not jump about, but he swiftly bent backwards, forwards and to each side so that his elbows almost touched the floor. One must remember that he acted thus in an era when musicians sat serenely on their chairs as they played. On the occasions when one member stood up to sing, he, (and it was always a "he") did so almost statue like with nothing moving but his lips. It can be truly said that in this regard John Fra was many years ahead of his time, as he apparently anticipated the gimmicks of showbands and rock bands with their antics and gyrations.

There were many other local bands about at that time and they were known by their leaders' names. One of them, described as Martin Conroy and His Melody Sextet had a great following from our area because the proprietor was born in Garryedmond gate lodge where he lived until his middle twenties. Other local band leaders included Jimmy Kearns, Kieran Ansboro, John Gallagher, Teddy Mack, Johnny Brady, Paddy Durkan and Matt McDonagh to mention but a few. In later years Matt McDonagh gave the name The Black Diamond to his band and others followed suit. Almost all band members dressed in full morning suits with black bow ties. I heard all of the foregoing and many others play over the next few years as I cycled with Jimmy to dances in Coogue, Bekan, Shanvahara, Pollavaddy and indeed further afield. We also attended dances in marquees and schools.

PURPOSE BUILT

In contrast to rural areas, few towns could boast of a purpose built dance hall in the thirties and the forties. For instance until Tom Foy built The New Savoy Ballroom which he owned jointly with Isaac Gannon, the only place for dancing in Claremorris was a large room in the old town hall which was itself a converted church. McGarry's Hall in Ballyhaunis was famous throughout South Mayo but it was simply a large converted store over a drapery shop. To gain access to it, a narrow stairs had to be ascended. The ceiling was low but it had an excellent floor and, more importantly, it had atmosphere. Every week there were columns of advertisements in *The Connaught Telegraph, The Western People* and *The Mayo News* drawing attention to the dances to be held on the following Sunday night throughout their circulation districts. The advertisements gave details of the band; the price of admission, and, wherever it was applicable, the last line in bold print emphasised that there was a polished maple floor.

Ballindine, situated about four miles from Claremorris and with a population of approximately two hundred, few of whom would be dance-goers, could boast of two purpose built dance halls. Even if they were primitive when compared with those built in later years in Tooreen, Ballyhaunis and the chain erected by the Reynolds brothers, in their own day they were very modern. These two halls were packed to the doors each Sunday night. One possible reason for the capacity crowds was the low admission fee of four old pence while the average charge in other halls was one shilling.

Most of those dances commenced at 10 p.m. and finished at 1 a.m. next morning. They were known as short dances. Others starting at the same time but finishing at 4 a.m. were long, or all night dances. There was a higher admission charge for the all night with more expensive, and more prestigious bands playing. These would include Mick Delahunty, Stephen Garvey and Des Fretwell. Other bands that started in a small way and quickly climbed into that category were those led and managed by Brose Walshe, Tony Chambers and Matt McDonagh. I am pleased to have had these three as personal friends and equally glad to relate that members of their families are carrying on the musical tradition with great success.

Perhaps the most famous Claremorris based band ever was that known as The Royal Blues. Managed by Andy Creighton it had among its personnel the Gill brothers from Murneen. It was an overnight success. Within a year of its inception in the fifties it was internationally known and it continued for a number of years playing in the United States and England as well as in every corner of Ireland.

ECLIPSING A TRADITION

A side effect of the change from country houses to dance halls was the eclipsing of another great rural tradition – that of matchmaking. Most romances now started in the dance hall. When a boy requested a girl to keep the next dance for him, or when he invited her to join him for a drink at the mineral bar it was only a step away from asking if he could see her to her home. If she agreed to keep the dance or if she accepted the drink it was an indication of a positive answer before the actual question was asked. Seeing the girl to her home was the equivalent of a match-making introduction. Marriage, of course, did not materialise on all occasions, but eventually most boys and girls met their marriage partners at dances.

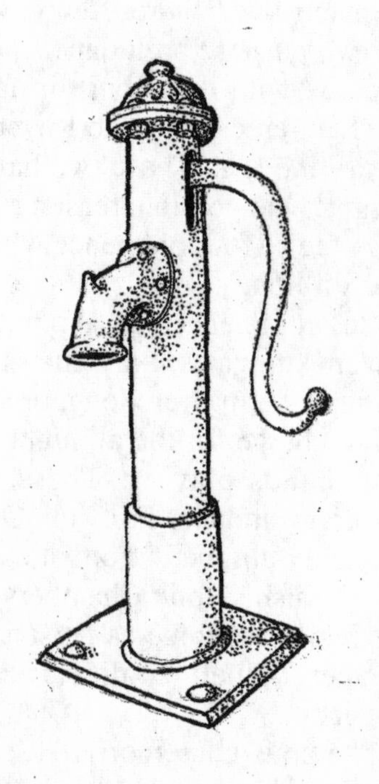

5

Matchmaking

INTRODUCING A PARTNER

To my knowledge there was never an official or recognised matchmaker in Garryedmond or in its surrounding area. Very definitely there was no professional member of the species about. But it was a pursuit in which all members of the community were prepared to indulge when the need arose, and they did so for the best of reasons.

Matchmaking took place mainly, if not entirely, among the rural community. If there was an eligible young farmer in one townland, and a neighbour or a relative of his knew of a young girl in another area, even several miles away, whom he believed would make a suitable partner for him, he would arrange an introduction. For the young farmer, being eligible meant that he had no brother or sister still living with him, and that his parents were willing to sign over the farm to him if they had not already done so. The girl to be eligible, had to have a certain amount of money which was called her "fortune," or more correctly her dowry. The larger the farm the more money was demanded in the dowry. Conversely, if the young girl had a large dowry there was no way that her family would allow her to marry into a small farm.

HER AGE WAS IMPORTANT

The age of the girl was more important than that of the man. Ideally she should not be more than twenty five. This was a time in our history when everybody wanted a large family, and up to age twenty-five it was assumed that she would have many years for childbearing. Despite the financial difficulties and hardships endured in rearing them, including the inconvenience of accommodating them in small houses where there were no modern amenities, society in general looked kindly and occasionally even enviously on large families.

The young parents looked forward to their children growing up, helping them to work on the land for a few years and then emigrating to America, from whence they hoped and indeed expected that dollars would arrive from them on a continual basis for the remainder of their lives. It was assumed that on arrival in America there was always work to be found accompanied by good wages. An uncle or an aunt usually lent the money for the passage of the first member of a family to cross the Atlantic. Having got employment, that member repayed the money and then saved enough to bring out the next brother or sister. They continued thus until the second last or third last emigrated, leaving one son at home to take over the farm, and sometimes a daughter who would, hopefully, marry into a neighbouring farm.

As the age of the girl was equal in importance to the size of the dowry it happened on occasions that a few years was deducted when she was being introduced to prospective husbands. Some held on to this secret until they applied for the Old Age Pension. I came across a few such cases myself, when, as a public representative, I was asked to make representations for a few years back payment for women who failed to apply until they were the age as stated when getting married. Unfortunately they were entitled to the pension only from the date of application.

MANNER OF INTRODUCTION

The manner of introduction in matchmaking was roughly the same in all cases. The person who knew both sides took on the role of matchmaker. He checked out the size of the man's farm and related matters such as the number of cattle, sheep and pigs thereon, and the amount of dowry required. He then called on the girl and her parents with this information, and if they were able and prepared to come up with the money or most of it, he arranged a meeting of both parties. This usually took place in a public house on a fair day and every pub had a private room for these meetings. Drinks were ordered and the members of each family were introduced by the matchmaker. If the young couple were happy enough with each other's appearance and manner then the first step was overcome. The next move was bargaining over the amount of the dowry, because like making a deal at a fair, the man's side always requested more money than they were prepared to accept while the girl's side offered less than they were prepared to give. When a compromise was reached a date was arranged for the girl's father and some close friend of his, usually a relative, to inspect the prospective groom's farm. This was referred to as "walking the land" and it normally took place on a Sunday.

At this point, as in the case of the girl's age, a certain amount of deception was not unknown. When showing the girl's father around the farm an extra field or two belonging to a neighbour was sometimes included with the connivance of the latter. And, as the number of cattle was sometimes exaggerated when bargaining over the dowry, it was often necessary to borrow a few for the day.

If the father of the bride-to-be was satisfied with the farm and stock the next step was a visit to a solicitor to draw up the marriage agreement, and then a call to the girl's parish priest. The marriage always took place in the parish of the bride. No notice was required, and often the marriage took place within a few weeks of the first meeting.

AN UNEXPECTED BRIDE

Occasionally the young couple only met for the second time in the church at the marriage ceremony. I have personally known a couple who were introduced in this way. The groom was waiting in the church at the appointed time, while the bride availed of a customary privilege of being a few minutes late. But the bride who arrived in this case was not the girl to whom the groom had been introduced, but her sister who was less good looking and who was regarded as being a little easy going. The first girl would have less difficulty in getting another man. Whether or not the groom appreciated the situation the marriage went ahead. He was a very honourable and God-fearing man who might well have assumed that this woman was destined for him. At any rate they lived a very long and most happy life together and although not blessed with children of their own, they could be said to be second parents to all the children of the district as well as to their own nieces and nephews. They were extremely popular and highly respected in the neighbourhood where they lived and died in the esteem of all who knew them.

A BROKEN MATCH

There was a match made between a girl from Garryedmond and a young farmer from near Milltown in Co. Galway. They had been introduced in the usual way and all concerned were apparently satisfied. The neighbours of the girl were delighted that she was getting married; they were invited to the wedding and some, including my own parents, had given her presents. The prospective groom for some reason had a change of heart. He could not inform the girl or her family of his decision, because at that stage he would be liable for breach of promise proceedings in the courts. And in such cases, which were indeed very rare, the family of the jilted girl was seldom slow to take action because success in obtaining damages was practically always assured. A jilted man on the other hand did not seem to have the same protection. In order to avoid litigation the Milltown man made careful plans. When members of the girl's family called on him to walk the land as previously arranged, instead of bringing in neighbour's cattle to boost his own herd he did the opposite. He put his best stock on a neighbour's farm and then scattered all sorts of litter around the house and farmyard, while within the dwelling it was as untidy as was possible. Sitting by the fire was an old woman wearing a shawl who stated that she was the man's crippled aunt who was permanently living there, but whose existence had not been revealed at the matchmaking introduction. Finally he showed signs of being a simpleton which were not evident at the first meeting. The girl's family figured that far from being a simpleton, he was a very clever man, and this conjecture was confirmed when a few months later they learned of his marriage to a local girl and the crippled aunt disappeared. They did not pursue the matter with litigation but the girl never married. She died many years ago at a ripe old age and as she was the last of her family there is now scarcely a trace of her old home.

IT'S ALL SO DIFFERENT NOW

Matchmaking or arranged marriages would be unthinkable in our modern society. But strange as it may seem broken marriages which are now part of everyday life were almost non existent half a century ago. If there were some who were unhappy, which of course there must have been, they accepted their lot mainly because of their deep and simple faith. But it was also true that they could not walk away from an unhappy union because there was nowhere to go. At that time there was no state allowance for separated people, and their parents or other members of their families were unlikely to be sympathetic towards them. Even if they were compassionate it is probable that they would not be in a position to accommodate them. People lived in frugality if not in poverty, and their only hope of survival lay in remaining together regardless of unhappiness. But it cannot be denied that practically all marriages were successful in those far off days, and if people had disputes they were minor ones, and they kept them within the walls of their own homes.

6

Knights of the Road

TRAMPS

Tramps or vagrants walking along the country roads were a common sight during my youth. No house was too remote for them to pay it a visit. Totally homeless and completely detached from family, relatives and friends, they were never asked from whence they came or how they happened to be penniless wanderers. People just accepted them as they were. Generally speaking their requirements were few and country people never denied them tea and buttered bread. If a vagrant was lucky enough to enter a house when the dinner was about to be served, an extra seat was provided at the table as was an equal share of whatever was going.

As the farmer always wore out his clothes to the point where they were threadbare and patched they were never asked for by the tramp who got the half worn jacket, trousers, shirt and shoes in the towns from business or professional people. Branches of organisations like the St. Vincent de Paul Society, where they existed, were not as well equipped to assist needy people as they are today. There was no help from the State such as dole and when old age and infirmity crept upon them and prevented a continuation of what was for them a normal way of life, the County Homes provided lonely but welcome refuge wherein to live out their remaining days. When the end came, unmarked paupers' graves awaited their mortal remains with no kith and kin to mourn them.

Although there were at least as many women begging as men, they always seemed to have some place to which they returned at night. This was usually a miserable, movable roadside tent, but as a rule there was a family group in it. All of them, including small children, went out begging each day. After staying only a few days in any area they picked up their tents which consisted of a few sticks and a sheet of canvas and moved on a few miles. This was their mode of existence throughout the whole year and throughout their whole lives.

Because of the constant movement it was not possible for the children to go to school even in the unlikely event of a desire for education being present. So like the generations that preceded them they grew up totally illiterate.

THEY SLEPT IN BARNS

Some of these vagrants came on a regular basis, maybe once or twice a year, and we knew them by name. Each usually carried a small sack slung across one shoulder within which was probably a change of underclothes. How they got those washed and dried I do not know and indeed it was something to which few people gave any thought at the time. If one arrived late on a Summer or Autumn evening he was likely to ask for permission to be allowed to sleep in the barn or granary. Such a request would never be refused. I have a clear recollection of a man named Micksie Curley arriving at our house one Winter night and my father brought in large armfuls of straw with which he made a shake down at the end of the kitchen. Had it been Summer or Autumn Micksie would have slept in the granary, where it is likely he would have been much happier. After his breakfast early next morning he immediately moved on, and where he stayed that night we neither knew nor cared. In fairness to those people it must be acknowledged that they did not ask for "lodgings" from the same householder again for many years, if ever. Although Micksie paid us a number of visits over the next few years he always came early in the day. We did, however, have other "lodgers" all of whom slept in the granary. They were never known to steal anything or do any kind of damage. The farming community were not just tolerant towards them – they had a certain respect and compassion for them as human beings.

A caller who slept regularly in our granary was Henry O'Brien. A native of Ballyhaunis district, he had at one stage been a clerical student and a Greek and Latin scholar. Somewhere along the line, following a mental breakdown, he took to the roads. However he always carried himself with dignity and there was understanding and tolerance for him wherever he went. On some of his visits he taught my brother the Greek alphabet.

TINKERS

Other categories of travellers roamed the countryside and probably the best known were the tinsmiths or tinkers. They made cans and saucepans from tin. This trade, which required a high degree of skill, was handed down from generation to generation. The women folk carried the finished products from house to house, offering them for sale, and they also brought them into the towns on the days of fairs and markets. Hardware merchants bought them in bulk at a cheaper rate so that they retailed them in their shops at the same prices as the tinsmith offered them to the public. The tinsmiths tried to earn their living in part at least but they also had recourse to begging. Having the proceeds from the tin products as an income enabled them to purchase horses and carts which in turn permitted them to travel further afield. This transport also gave them the added comfort of carrying their wares and having to do less walking themselves. It cost nothing to feed the horses as they grazed on the roadside grass which was known as the long acre. In time many of those tinkers or tinsmiths began to deal in horses and eventually to breed them.

GYPSIES

The gypsies were, and still are, of a different ilk and culture. They appeared to be reasonably affluent, having had gaily decorated horse drawn caravans which were expensively furnished, and some contained priceless antiques. Horse dealers and breeders long before the tinkers got involved in that business, they also purchased rugs, carpets and linoleum from wholesalers and manufacturers, and those items were offered for sale around the country as they hawked them from house to house.

Gypsies are believed to be descended from nobility. Among themselves they still speak the language of the Romany tribe to which they belong. On the other hand the tinkers' forebears were in many cases Irish men and women who were evicted from their homes by ruthless and callous landlords in penal times because they were unable to pay their rents.

PAT KILLEEN

Garryedmond was the birthplace of one Pat Killeen who, having fallen down on his luck, forsook the normal rural way of life and became a beggar. An only child who was born in a thatched cottage near the railway gatehouse about 1890, he was apprenticed to the bar and grocery trade in Ballyhaunis while in his teens. Having fallen victim to drink which resulted in him losing his job, he spent the remainder of his long life trudging through the streets of that town playing a tin whistle and asking for alms.

While working in Ballyhaunis he found an ingenious way of getting free lifts to his home in Garryedmond. Back in the days of the steam engines, on leaving a station, a train travelled several hundred yards before gathering speed. Pat waited a short distance from the station and he hopped on to the buffer of the final carriage of the first train to go by, and there he sat until it reached the upward slope near his home. As the engine lacked the power of the modern diesel it was forced to slow down on every hill, thereby enabling Pat to jump off in reasonable safety almost beside his parents' house. There is no record of how he travelled the seven miles back to Ballyhaunis after those visits.

Pat Killeen was a polite, harmless individual and one of the best known characters in Ballyhaunis for many decades. His whole adult life was spent in that town where he lived in a state of frugality in the less than pleasant surroundings of The Dardanelles.

MUSICIANS

There was the odd musician who travelled through several counties going from door to door in rural Ireland. The last of those who was calling to Garryedmond for many years and whose name I cannot now recall played the bagpipes. He was a regular visitor until the late fifties. It is doubtful if any of them were very talented and the music was simply a means of introduction. It also gave them a feeling of self respect as they were offering something in return for the alms they hoped to collect.

PEDLARS

In a similar manner some women offered for sale small items unwanted by people but which they still purchased. They included clothes pegs, hair clips and camphor balls. These were easy to carry and were usually peddled by women who lived in towns and who strolled out through the country during the long summer days, but always returned to their homes at night. Those pedlars were generous in praying for God's blessing on their benefactors, but if abused or turned away without receiving some charity they could be equally as bountiful with their curses.

One old lady, a real tartar, who was peddling all her life was a frequent visitor to our district and she knew every family by name. On entering a house she was likely to make reference to a few neighbours, describing them as decent people. Obviously they had given her a glass of whiskey or a few shillings. There were others, however, whose identity she subtly revealed without a mention of their names in whose company she would not be seen dead. Apart from referring to their miserliness there might be a hint of some scandal in the family which was not publicly known. The message was clear. "Treat me generously and I will praise you in other houses but do the opposite and I will scandalise you." It was a good strategy, because while people did not believe her calumnious stories, they treated her kindly to ensure that she did not speak adversely about themselves. Her practice in this regard could be compared with that of the bards in Brehon times, who if belittled by the elite, turned the tables on their detractors by composing disparaging songs about them.

MONK ROGERS

An unusual, if not unique, traveller was a man known as Monk Rogers who always dressed in what appeared to be clerical garb. Suit, overcoat, vest and hat were all black and to complete the impersonation a Roman collar adorned his neck. Many people believed that he had once been a monk in a monastery or had at least been a seminarian. But as his history remained a mystery, any assumption concerning him was based on conjecture. He offered for sale a variety of small religious objects, mainly pictures, medals and rosaries, and being very business-like, he had little difficulty in disposing of them. They were inexpensive and it was as easy to buy something from him as to give him a monetary donation which indeed he might not accept because throughout his life he kept up the pretence of being a cleric, and resented any insinuation that he was a beggar.

He was known to look for accommodation in rural houses, usually calling after darkness fell, and explaining that he was on missionary work in the locality and the car from the monastery which was to collect him, had failed to arrive. Because of the respect in which priests were held, his victims felt honoured to oblige him and no difficulty arose until he became known in a district. He was very demanding with regard to food, and before retiring, requested his hosts to have toast and two boiled brown eggs prepared for his breakfast. When only white eggs were available he became agitated and refused to accept them.

His only overnight stay in Garryedmond was in the house of Maggie Prendergast who was given the usual culinary instruction. Believing he was a priest she was mortified to discover that her basket contained only white eggs, but she quietly slipped a lump of soot into the saucepan and when boiled, the eggs were brown. Most likely that story would not have been revealed had she not discovered that he was a fake.

Monk Rogers was known to have travelled extensively throughout Mayo, North Galway and Roscommon, but he spent most of his life in the latter county.

OTHER TYPES

There were indeed many other types of knights of the road from Jack the Papers to herring sellers to the collectors of bottles and rags. They had much in common but were at the same time individualistic and all added life and colour to the rural Ireland of those times. They inspired poets and writers for centuries. Tales of Kitty the Hare, and songs like The Homes of Donegal and The Beggerman, appeared to glamourise the life, but the reality was different.

Among them too were many people of genius like the gifted artists Turlough O'Carolan, Antoine Raftery and Padraic O'Conaire, who left their homes for whatever reason and took to life on the roads.

Words like beggars, tramps and tinkers are no longer used because they are considered offensive by all right-thinking people – especially travellers themselves, who are entitled to the dignity of descriptions acceptable to them.

7

Sports

CIVIC MINDED PEOPLE

During the decade prior to the Second World War a Sports Committee seemed to spring up in every parish in rural Ireland. They were organised by civic minded people who had the well-being of their locality at heart. The main aims of those committees were to provide the local youth with a healthy outlet for energy and to give entertainment to adults who came in large numbers to see them perform on Sunday afternoons throughout the summer.

A valuable side effect was the substantial amount of money which was collected from entrance fees received from the contestants plus the admission charges from the patrons. This money was used to further some local project such as purchasing a field for football and then if required, fencing, draining or levelling it.

CASTLEGAR BALL ALLEY

A Sports Committee in my parish built a ball alley in Castlegar in the nineteen thirties and it provided a venue for hundreds of young men and boys to learn, practise and enjoy the game of handball over a period of thirty years. It also served as a meeting place for scores of people of all age groups on Sunday afternoons and during the long mid-week evenings in Summer. Situated about two miles from Claremorris on the Knock road, it was an ideal distance from the town which has now expanded almost as far as it. But at that time when transport was either a bicycle or shanks mare it comprised an activity away from the pubs and from the less vigorous indoor entertainment of billiards, snooker and card playing in the Town Hall.

A DRAMA GROUP

The cost of building the ball alley was paid mainly from money raised at sports meetings. The committee consisted of energetic and enthusiastic people and the whole community so appreciated their endeavours that they were only too willing to help them in any way possible. For instance in an effort to raise funds a number of young people led by Patrick Morley from Cloontooa formed a drama group and they staged a play. Various audiences, mainly in school houses throughout South and East Mayo, enjoyed the production. Apart from the monetary result, they had the pleasure of giving entertainment to many, and it fostered a spirit of comradeship among themselves which taking part in drama has an uncanny way of doing.

PERRY

The members of the committee were young local people most of whom have now passed to their rewards. Practically all of the men thereon played handball and many of them became expert at the game. Among them was a cousin of mine, Jim Egan, who was a most popular young man.

At that time the champion hand ball player was Paddy Perry. Partnered usually by Paddy McGuinness, Jim Egan's exploits in the alley were a treat to watch. So skilled did he become in the game that he was inevitably compared with Paddy Perry. In games when he killed ball after ball from what seemed impossible angles the cheers from the onlookers re-echoed from the walls. When a ball was coming to him there were shouts of "Come on Perry" and when he killed or butted it the roar

REANEY'S MILL

was "Good man Perry." In a short while he became affectionately known as Perry Egan and in due course many people who later became his close acquaintances were unaware of his correct Christian name.

The field where the annual sports were held was owned by the Reaney family who generously allowed the committee to use it each year. They were a most civic-minded family whose worth to the local community was scarcely fully appreciated. They ran a small grocery shop and their home, whose doors were open to every caller, was the local visiting house. Progressive and enterprising, they operated a grinding mill powered by the current of a nearby river. The pristine building with the old mill-wheel still attached, stands today as a monument to a vanished era.

CASTLEGAR SPORTS

The sports field as we called it was such for only one day each year. Ideally situated along the main Claremorris-Knock road it was comparatively small, comprising of approximately two acres. Around the perimeter was a sod fence on which grew a thick hawthorn edge which was about ten feet high, so there was no way that the events could be viewed from the road. Anyway adults came to support the committee and to enjoy themselves while most youngsters wanted to participate in the sports. Within that field on one Sunday each Summer there was great excitement which you sensed as you paid your shilling at the gate and heard the hawkers shout "Apples, oranges and ripe bananas." Their stands were loaded with fruit, sweets, chocolates and lemonade.

As a small child I walked the two miles to Castlegar from my home, always accompanied by my brother Séamus. As we passed by my aunt's house she never failed to bring us in and give us a half crown each. That was big money at the time which more than equalled the amount we got from our parents when we were leaving home earlier.

Along the way we were joined by neighbouring children all of whom we knew. Many of them attended Koilmore National School with us. Most of us took part in some of the competitions such as the sack race; the three legged race; the egg and spoon race and other races like the hundred yards sprint confined to under ten years or under twelve years as the case might be. I do not remember what the prizes were, the main reason being that I seldom won any.

During the years that followed, again accompanied by my brother and one or two neighbours I cycled to sports meetings in Hollymount, Boleyboy, Crossboyne, Bekan and Knock. We cycled to patterns at Ballyhaunis Friary and we even went to one held adjacent to the ruins of Urlaur Abbey near Kilmovee. Although now young adults and mere spectators we still took great interest in weight throwing, the long and high jumps, cycle races and pony races all of which were very competitive. Many of the contestants became friends of ours as they too went from sports to sports in an effort to win as many prizes as possible.

TUG-O-WAR

Of special significance to us was the Tug-o-War competition be - cause Castlegar team ruled the roost in the region for many years. The team members were all neighbours and we were there to cheer them on. Tug-o-War was a test of strength and skill by a team of seven men against another team of a similar number, pulling a heavy rope of about two inches in diameter and approximately twenty one yards long. The rope, with a loop on each end, was laid out full length on the ground and tied in its centre was a long piece of ribbon. About two feet to each side of the centre were two shorter pieces of ribbon.

The heaviest man on each team entered the loop which he made sure fitted comfortably around his waist. They put a slight strain on the rope which lifted it a couple of feet off the ground. Then the six other men from each team took hold of the rope at about three feet apart. This left a space of about two yards each side of the long ribbon which had to be directly over a permanent mark on the ground. The referee stood at the centre and when both teams were ready he called out "Hold the strain." When he was satisfied that the long ribbon was exactly over the mark he gave the order "Pull." It was not simply a matter of one team pulling against the other. A coach stood close to the front man on his team and through some skill or intuition he seemed to know the right moment to order his men to jerk the rope. He then shouted "Heave." The order, like that of a conductor of an orchestra, ensured that all jerked or heaved together and if they succeeded in moving the other team even an inch or two they were likely to get the upper hand. Of course the opposition also had a coach giving similar orders to his men, so where the teams were evenly matched in strength and weight the result depended on the expertise of the coach. There was no time limit for the contest but the struggle was so strenuous it seldom lasted more than a few minutes. The team had won when they had pulled the rope to the point where the short ribbon furthest from them crossed the mark on the ground.

When the Castlegar team was going well the coach was Dick Nally from Cartownacross. He was then a man of late middle age who was extremely popular and regarded as one of the best in the business. When every other coach used the term "Heave" Dick used his own personal words of command "Up and Away."

There was so much talent available in Castlegar district that occasionally they fielded a second team. Tug-o-War was a most enjoyable spectator sport especially when the team one supported was winning. It was perhaps less pleasant for the contestants who had to dress in old clothes and heavy boots. They often lost their footing and then fell to the ground which was likely to be torn and sometimes wet and mucky. However, as in all amateur games, the honour of representing their districts was uppermost in their minds and was in itself a reward even if a trophy eluded them or if they got soaked in slush to win it.

THE ATHLETE FROM AGHAMORE

At one particular sports meeting in the late nineteen forties a young athlete from Aghamore won the first prizes in cycling, running and the long jump. By the time he was competing in the high jump he knew that because of his success there was great resentment against him. The height in the first round was fairly low so all contestants cleared it. Each succeeding round saw the lath risen by an inch or two while the umpire publicly announced the exact height. Little by little contestants were eliminated until there remained only two and one of them was the athlete from Aghamore. When a height was reached that the other contestant failed to clear, the umpire when replacing the lath, announced that it was set again at the same ceiling. The Aghamore man however was suspicious and on checking the measurement found that it was placed two inches higher for him. They had hot words but it was then placed at the correct height and he cleared it easily. Although now the winner he insisted on the lath being put up the extra two inches and he cleared that also. But because of the incident he did not compete again which was regrettable because without people like him there would be no sports meetings at all. This athlete's name was Michael Cuddy and he became a prominent business man in Claremorris in later years.

DEBBIE.

Castlegar ball alley was brought down by Debbie, the big storm in 1961. It was never replaced, although a modern covered-in alley was built in the town later. It has nostalgic memories for many natives of the area who settled both in Ireland and in far distant parts of the world. For me personally it provided the opportunity to play the only athletic game in which I had a reasonable measure of success even if I did not excel at it. The availability of the ball alley was all the more important because of the absence of a football team or pitch in the area. We did however, regularly play our own brand of Gaelic games among the small number at our disposal, and we were never denied the use of their fields by four most generous neighbours all of whom have passed on, namely John Foy, Jim Dunleavy, Mike Cunnane and Michael Fleming. The latter actually "togged out" with us occasionally.

The ball alley was also the venue where members of the Local Security Force and Local Defence Force met about three nights per week during the Emergency for drilling operations. I will always remember with gratitude that the officer in charge allowed me to take part in the drill when I was too young to join the force. Eventually I was accepted, and indeed one of my fondest possessions is my service medal.

Many of those who were members of the Defence Forces at that time as well as hundreds who played handball in the ball alley or even participated in the Pitch and Toss schools outside it, and the countless numbers who were involved with the Sports either as participants or spectators in the days of my youth are gone. For those of us who are still about, Castlegar with Reaney's shop, the ball alley and the sports field will always have a special place in our memories.

8

Religion

SUNDAY MASS

Religion and religious beliefs played a big part in the lives of all Catholics in Ireland in the thirties and forties. This was particularly true in the rural areas. Nothing, barring serious illness or infirmity, would prevent anybody from going to Mass on Sundays or Holydays of Obligation. When storms, frost or snow made it impossible to cycle or to bring horses with traps or side cars on the roads the people simply walked. If they returned to their homes worn out by exhaustion, blue with the cold, or drenched from the rain, they did not complain. It would never dawn on them to neglect what they believed to be their religious duties. Priests at the time made it clear that to assist at Mass was not obligatory in such circumstances but they would have felt uncomfortable, if not guilty, had they stayed at home. In every house each day was brought to a close with the recitation of the rosary.

SODALITIES

Practically all adults were members of the Sodality. They were expected to go to Confession once a month and to receive Holy Communion at the first Mass on their allotted Sunday. In our parish the centre of the church was reserved for the Children of Mary at the first Mass on the first Sunday of each month. It was reserved for members of the men's sodality on the second Sunday and for those of the women's sodality on the third. Children who had already received their first Holy Communion had their own day on the fourth Sunday but at second Mass.

Each street in the town, and roughly each Station area in the country, had its own branches of men's and women's Sodalities which were called guilds. Each guild had one member in charge. This person was appointed by the parish priest and was carefully selected on the basis of his/her known piety and respectability within the community. The assignment was held for life or until old age or incapacity rendered it impossible to carry on. The duties of the office entailed collecting the small token membership fee and to note and report to the parish priest if any member was straying from the obligations of membership. I never heard of such reports but that does not say that some were not made. What action the priest would take in such a situation is debatable but in all probability he would discreetly contact the person concerned to find out the reason for the diminishing interest, and then inveigle a return to the straight and narrow path towards salvation.

Seats were allocated in the centre of the Church to each Sodality guild in accordance with the number of members therein. They could range from three to six or seven. Each guild was under the patronage of a saint whose name and image were depicted on a banner assigned to it. This banner, which also had a number on it, stood loftily over the first of the seats allocated, and the members took their places behind it. To hold the banners upright, brass rings were screwed to the seats and they are still to be seen in some churches.

Dr. George Maguire acted as M.C. on the men's day and he ensured that each row of seats emptied one by one from the front of the church as they went to the rails to receive Holy Communion. In a most impressive and dignified way he maintained complete order.

SAINT COLMAN

John Foy was head of the men's guild for Garryedmond area, which like Claremorris parish was under the patronage of Saint Colman, who in the Middle Ages, built a church in the townland of Kilcolman which is situated about four miles from Claremorris on the Kiltimagh road. The ruins lie within the graveyard which is now largely disused for burials.

It is strange that there are comparatively few boys named after St. Colman in the parish. Certainly when compared with the number of Jarlaths in Tuam, Brendans in Loughrea, Aidans in Wexford and Finbarrs in Cork, he can scarcely be described as getting the recognition that is his due. In other spheres, however, he is better commemorated. Claremorris parish church is dedicated to him as is the new cemetery on the Balla road. St. Colman's College, which was founded in the forties, has probably done most to keep his name alive because of the thousands of students who have passed through its doors and also by reason of the remarkably successful results achieved there both academically and in the field of Gaelic Football. A number of business people have also put their premises under his patronage. An early establishment was William O'Keeffe's *Kilcolman Press* which was followed by Michael Reidy's *Kilcolman Housing Society.* Vincent Donnellan built *St. Colman's Funeral Home* which was among the first in Mayo, and the eminently successful *St. Colman's Credit Union* embellishes the town with its imposing building in The Square.

EUCHARISTIC PROCESSIONS

To return briefly to the Sodality banner, it was also used at another important ceremony. It was carried by the head of the guild as he led his members in the Eucharistic procession which took place each year on the feast of Corpus Christi. In parishes where processions still take place, there is no banner because there is no Sodality as we knew it. Its demise is due mainly to the fact that Holy Communion is now distributed at all Masses whereas before Vatican II adults received only at the first Mass each Sunday.

The Procession was a moving and impressive ceremony at which everybody from the smallest child to the oldest person walked and behaved in a most reverential manner. It was an event to which all children looked forward and it was a topic of conversation for weeks afterwards. Marching at the front were members of the local branch of the Legion of Mary, followed by the church choir, then the girls from the schools of the parish followed by the boys, then the women's and men's sodality guilds, the altar boys carrying lighted candles and finally a priest holding aloft the monstrance from which the Blessed Sacrament could be seen. A canopy was held over him by six men, three on either side, and they walked in step with him. The canopy bearers were teachers and local business people. It was regarded as a great honour to be selected to carry it and those so favoured continued in office until death or infirmity overtook them.

Windows and doorways along the procession route were decorated with statues, blessed pictures and lighted candles while papal and national flags flew from public buildings. A guard of honour, usually provided by the gárdai, marched outside the canopy bearers. The procession proceeded from the Church through the exit leading to Mount Street. It turned left for the Square, then right as far as the end of James Street and back to the Square where an altar had been erected. Everybody knelt there for Benediction.

The Procession was now regarded as over but most of the people walked with the priest, still carrying the Blessed Sacrament under the canopy, as he led the way for the short distance back to the church. In parishes where the Annual Procession is still preserved the format has changed but little.

THE MISSION

Every three years there was a mission in our parish. While some were conducted by Passionists, Jesuits and Carmelites it was more usual to have Redemptorists. The latter were regarded as the toughest because they put the fear of God into people with their fire and brimstone sermons. Despite, or perhaps because of the terror generated by them, Redemptorists were still the most popular of missioners and the more fright engendered the better the mission was regarded. Sermons apart, they were very pleasant and good humoured when one met them down town or in the Church and their funny stories were always well received, especially those they told against themselves.

There was one week for the women and one for the men. The sermons preached for each sex were almost exactly the same but this arrangement made it easier for both parents to attend, especially where there were small children. Moreover the Church would not be big enough to contain the congregation if there were not separate sessions.

Nearly every morning for the duration of the mission the Church was full for the special Mass which was celebrated at 7 a.m., and again for the night ceremonies at which the main sermon was preached. The Wednesday night sermon was sure to be extra well attended especially by young, single people, because it dealt with the then cardinal sin of company keeping. This sermon was the most interesting but also the most chilling because practically all young persons listening felt that, unless they changed their ways, damnation was very near. Of course that did not apply to those who were married or were of a rare species who never kept company and never had thoughts concerning the opposite sex.

The Wednesday night sermon sent queues of youths scurrying to Confessions the next day after which there was a real sense of relief on being shriven. Romances sometimes broke up as a result of a sermon. Dating was definitely out for the duration, but human nature ensured that before long things were back to normal again.

People may laugh nowadays at the acquiescence of the community in those times, but it must be conceded that the missions did a lot of good in that they gave relief and solace to many even if this did not always endure. Although the missioners were hard in their sermons they still succeeded in giving consolation in the confessional.

THE POWER OF THE PRIEST

People had great belief in the power of priests and they accepted without question the authenticity of stories concerning them. They seemed to confuse the power vested in them with regard to the Sacraments with their positions as human beings. I believed far-fetched stories told to me during my childhood by adults who themselves believed them. One concerned an argument between a priest and a parishioner. It became so heated that the latter lost his temper and was attempting to strike the priest when to his horror he found that he could no longer move. With fist still clenched his rigid position remained until he made an apology. This the priest accepted and mobility returned immediately.

The friars in Ballinasmalla Abbey were, according to local legend, out saving a large field of hay on their farm one sunny Summer day when suddenly it began to rain. They feared that their crop would be ruined so they knelt down and prayed. The rain fell in torrents everywhere around but not in their hayfield. There the sun shone until the crop was secured.

Perhaps those and myriad similar stories are true but if they were told to a child of eight or ten years today it is unlikely they would be believed.

James Murphy, our teacher, never advised us to believe or disbelieve those legends but one of his many funny stories may reflect his thinking. During the time when priests' only mode of transport was horseback the local curate dismounted outside a shop in the town. Seeing a young boy nearby he called him over and instructed him to hold the horse until he returned from the shop.

The boy refused. Shocked at such insolence the priest asked him "Do you know who I am and are you aware of the power that I possess? I could stick you to the ground."

"If that is true," replied the boy, "why don't you stick the horse to the ground?"

BALLINASMALLA ABBEY

The ruins of Ballinasmalla Abbey are now partially restored and Mass was offered there by Carmelite Fathers on July 27th, 1984 and once every year since. The Abbey, which was founded in 1288 and served the local community continually until 1870 when Father Simon J. Carr, the last priest to live there, left it. Most people passing by, or attending funerals in the graveyard which surrounds it and which is officially closed except for the last of a family, might think that the church was unused for some hundreds of years. However my grandfather, John Costello who died in 1924 attended Mass there throughout his youth. Within the graveyard are buried several generations of my family. They include my brother, aunt, parents, grandparents and great grandparents.

THE STATIONS

The custom of having the Stations still continues in much the same way as in my youth. A difference is that there is less need for preparation nowadays, because all houses have up to date facilities and appliances and they are kept in good decorative condition all the time. It is a far cry from the setting that pertained in the thirties and forties. While most farmers, or their wives, whitewashed their kitchens and the outer walls of their houses once a year, a total overhaul took place only with the approach of the Stations. This meant that all ceilings, doors and windows had to be washed down and painted. In fact everything made of timber, including the partitions, kitchen table, chairs, dresser and the chiffonier which was an essential in every house succumbed to the paint brush. Stations time was boom time for hardware merchants when sales of paints, brushes and kitchen utensils soared. To a lesser extent furniture sales increased also.

With the exception of the loft, no place in the house was private on the day of the Stations. Houses with parlours were few and far between, so early in the morning the bed was taken out of the larger bedroom which then became a sitting room cum dining room for the day. New linoleum had been laid on the bedroom floors while the concrete floor in the kitchen had been scrubbed clean on the previous day and carefully swept on the morning. When the kitchen was whitewashed the bedroom walls got a coat or two of distemper. As well as the outside of the house, gate pillars were whitewashed or cement-washed and if there was a barn or carthouse to the front of the dwelling the walls got a coat also. Some went so far as to paint the galvanised iron roofs of the outoffices and of course all gates were painted. Streets, which would today be called driveways, were cleaned and they got a spread of sand.

Two priests arrived at approximately 8.30 on the morning accompanied by the sacristan or parish clerk. The women would be already in the house while the men waited outside chatting among themselves until the arrival of the priests. All went into the house then and both priests commenced hearing Confessions immediately. One went to the bedroom where a fireside chair, probably a brand new one, awaited him, while the other remained in the kitchen. In the meantime the sacristan opened the vestments box within which were also the sacred vessels, and he prepared the altar. This box had been delivered on the previous evening by the people in whose house the Station Mass had been celebrated the morning before.

Confessions over, one priest proceeded to celebrate Mass while the other visited the sick people in the Station area, to hear their confessions and give them Holy Communion. He usually arrived back just as the Mass and sermon were over. With the sacristan they had breakfast in the Station house and were sometimes joined by the man of the house or by some neighbour whom the householders particularly wished to honour. After breakfast the priests chatted for about ten minutes with the people before taking their departure.

Most of the women and some of the men waited for breakfast. Some women stayed on to help with washing up and to prepare for visitors, mainly relatives who would continue to call throughout the day.

Sometime during the afternoon the man of the house tackled the horse or ass and cart, and on to it he loaded the vestments box which he delivered to the house in the next townland where the Stations would be held on the following day.

As night approached all the young people (and some not so young) from the neighbourhood came for the dance which, over the years, had become part of the festivity associated with the Stations. A good meal was provided for all present after which they enjoyed music and dancing until the early hours of the morning.

FIRST COMMUNION AND CONFIRMATION

As children we walked to Mass in Brickens Church each Sunday. It was not in our parish but it was less than half the distance to Claremorris. Our parents cycled to Mass in the town.

Whatever the situation was for those going to Mass in the town there was certainly no fuss made about First Communion for the children who worshipped in Brickens. I made my First Confession and received my first Holy Communion on the same day at the Stations in McNieve's house in Garryedmond. There was no party nor any kind of celebration of the event. I did not get a certificate nor even a medal as a memento. Perhaps that is the way it should be. There is undoubtedly too much frenzy today and the sacrament would appear to be secondary but there should be a middle ground. I certainly would have liked if a little more had been made of the occasion.

Confirmation was different. There were children present from every school in the parish. We all had new suits, shirts and shoes. It meant two days off from school. On the first day we took our places in the Church under the watchful eyes of the teachers, to be examined by the Bishop on our knowledge of Christian doctrine. His questions were simple which was a relief because we had been led to expect otherwise. On the second day the Sacrament was administered. Afterwards we stayed in the town for a few hours spending the money which had been given to us in the manner that children will always spend it on such occasions.

THE PRIESTS' MONEY

In years gone by what are known today as the Christmas, Easter and Autumn dues were described as "the priests' money." The head of the men's sodality was also the collector of dues in his own area. It was probably a task that most adults did not relish and it took up quite an amount of time. For a youngster it was different and it was my luck to be living next door to John Foy who was the official collector. For many years until his own sons, Paddy and John, grew big enough to do the job he asked me to collect for him, and I revelled in the assignment. Knowing all the people and having the opportunity of calling on them in their homes made the task a pleasant social occasion which would not have come my way only for the dues. An added enticement at Christmas was the anticipation of plum pudding and lemonade in many houses.

It sometimes took me three evenings to finalise the collection, as some people would not be at home and others might tell me to call on Friday night after the eggler passed. The eggler was a provision merchant who, in his horse and cart, travelled on a regular weekly basis from house to house through the country. He purchased whatever amount of eggs the farmer's wife had for sale, and then she bought most of her groceries for the coming week from him. In later years when egg farming became obsolete the merchants continued to call with groceries and provisions. They had become mechanised by then and their lorries became known as travelling shops. After the grocery bill was paid there was a substantial balance due to the housewife. This was her housekeeping money for the remainder of the week, which served to buy other necessities and it covered incidental expenses like the priests' money.

Eventually having completed the collection I delivered it to John Foy together with a list of the people and the amounts they had paid. It was in walking, or rather cycling, order but before remitting the cash to the parish priest he compiled his own list using a different criterion. At the top he placed the name of the person who had paid the largest amount of money and continued with the second largest and so on down to the least. This was the way that he and the other collectors were expected to write them if not actually so instructed.

The reason was that each list was read separately from the pulpit on Sunday after Sunday at the last Masses following Christmas and Easter until the last subscription was announced. One might expect this to be boring, but it was absorbed with greater attention than any sermon ever preached with the possible exception of the one on company-keeping at the mission, and the concentration was so intense that the proverbial dropping of a pin could almost be heard.

The amount paid by farmers varied but little from collection to collection. During the years of my involvement, a few at the top paid five shillings; the next paid four shillings and a few paid half a crown. There was never a question of anybody not paying. It was treated as a lawful demand on their resources or incomes similar to the rates or land annuities. The amount paid was never less than that of the previous collection and if they made any alteration, it was an upward one.

In contrast to their country cousins, many shopkeepers in the town vied with each other to head the list in their own street. The names at the top changed often as one tried to outdo another, and an unexpected rise to the summit would be a topic of conversation throughout the parish for weeks afterwards.

Priests in general detested having to read them but like everybody else in those days they had difficulty in making ends meet. However, reading the lists could be regarded as a form of intimidation.

On one occasion a curate in our parish broke with tradition and he read out the Autumn lists which was not normally done. The difference in the amounts paid in comparison to those of Christmas and Easter was an eye opener. He did this only once which might suggest that the subscribers got the message so he did not need to do it again.

The Autumn collection was referred to as "oats money." This description came from the time that priests' only mode of travel was on horseback, and after the farmers harvested and threshed their corn they gave a bag of oats to the priests for their horses.

THE BARRIERS

When St. Colman's Parish Church was built in 1908 it cost a lot of money which left the parish in debt for many years. It was, and still is, a magnificent structure and following renovations in 1995, costing approximately half a million pounds, it is now more majestic than ever. Among the recent alterations were the provision of a Blessed Sacrament Chapel which doubles as a cry chapel on Sundays and Holydays; improvement at the entrance doors and the removal of the pulpit.

There were occasional changes over the years as when the high altar was moved to comply with Vatican II directions and the installation of electric light and later central heating. In order to accommodate the heating radiators it was necessary to remove ornate wooden barriers that separated the main centre aisle from the two side aisles. Those barriers had served a purpose when the Church was built of which few people today would be aware. In order to collect money to help in paying off the building debt, everybody who used the centre aisle during Sunday Masses was expected to pay two pennies at the door. Those who went in the left aisle were to pay one penny while the right aisle was free. Although the custom of paying fixed amounts at different doors had vanished long before the removal of the barriers, the left and right side aisles were still respectively referred to as "the penny side," and "the free side," during my youth.

KNOCK

There is an old saying "the nearer the Church the further from God" but in Claremorris it was an adage that did not apply where Knock was concerned for it was always regarded as a great privilege to be living in a parish adjoining such a hallowed place.

People walked from all around us in their hundreds to ceremonies in Knock not alone on Sundays but on most days throughout the pilgrimage season. They walked there in much greater numbers to the all-night vigils especially on the eve of August 21st which is the anniversary of the Apparition of the Blessed Virgin there in 1879 and the tradition still continues. If some might think that the walk is a form of entertainment or that there is no penance attached to it, they should meet people on their return from a vigil after being awake throughout the night in prayer, and having completed the fourteen miles on foot. Although suffering from blistered feet and general exhaustion they refuse lifts from generous motorists as they resolutely complete the journey.

My home was less than five miles from Knock, but my long-held ambition to take part in an all-night vigil was never realised. However, I often cycled there on Sundays each Summer as did my parents and

KNOCK SHRINE

many of our neighbours. For our family it was an extra pleasant tour through Cloontooa and Cloonfaughna, for we combined visits to many of our relatives in that district with our pilgrimages. My paternal grandmother was one of a very large family, all of whom were born in Rookfield where four generations onward her kinfolk, the Jordan family, still reside, and as most of them married locally we now have numerous cousins living in that neighbourhood. They include the families of Guilfoyles, Byrnes, McDonaghs, Morleys, Healys, Grogans, Fagans, Mulkeens, Reddingtons and probably many more.

When living in Claremorris I had the privilege of working as a steward at Knock Shrine for a number of seasons. This was a moving experience, giving me an insight into much suffering borne so patiently by so many invalids. Despite the fact that some physical hardship was not unknown to me personally in my earlier years, as I had known the inside of an orthopaedic ward of a hospital for a long time, their acceptance still amazed me. One could not fail to be impressed too by the huge number of people from all walks of life who gave their time, expertise and commitment so generously in helping the sick at the Shrine. John Jordan was Chief Steward when I joined the ranks. A short time before that the position was held by Joe Blowick from Belcarra who was a T.D. and on two occasions Minister for Lands. Afterwards, when I joined him as a colleague on Mayo Co. Council we became great friends and it was a pleasure to have known him as he was a gentleman to his finger tips. There were many stewards and handmaids from Claremorris there at that time and the same position applies today.

Any reference to Knock would be incomplete if it did not allude to the late Monsignor James Horan, and indeed his praises have been sung throughout the world. He made history when he arranged for the first ever visit of a Pope to Ireland. This was in 1979 when John Paul II came for the centenary celebrations in Knock. The Monsignor and an excellent committee built the basilica and the international airport that bears his name. He had a turbulent time trying to get the airport established but he got help from friends in high places. He publicly acknowledged the assistance received from the then Taoiseach and former Mayo Person of the Year, Charles Haughey, and at local level from parishioner P. J. Morley T.D. They were strongly supported by the Environment Minister, Padraig Flynn, who later became E.U.

Commissioner, by Jim Higgins, a Junior Minister and by Martin Finn, a former T.D. who sacrificed much because of his efforts on behalf of Knock. Allowing for this assistance and that of his countless friends throughout the world the achievements of Monsignor Horan were still nothing short of miraculous. Anybody who has seen the transformation of Knock in such a short time from what could be described as a shanty village to a modern town; the erection of the magnificent basilica and an international airport where there was a mere bog, must suspect that he received help from friends in a place higher still.

CROAGH PATRICK

The annual pilgrimage to Croagh Patrick which, like Knock, nestles within our beloved Mayo was a must for most young people in the West. It was over thirty miles from my home yet I succeeded in climbing it eight times in successive years. On each of those occasions I was accompanied by Tom Keane of Cloontooa. Others to join in our group over these years included Brian Byrne, Bertie Murray, Jim Morley, Billy McGagh and Paddy Callaghan.

We always climbed the mountain at night and commenced our descent immediately after the first Mass on the summit. This was celebrated on an altar in a glass covered annex to the chapel. Although viewing Clew Bay on the downward trek as dawn broke was both breathtaking and gratifying, our arrival at Murrisk brought a sigh of relief from all of us. Tired and weary we always were, but also invigorated from having completed another successful pilgrimage.

Croagh Patrick has been internationally known for centuries as a place of pilgrimage but it it also a place of great archaeological interest. Excavations by archaeologists Gerry Walsh and Michael Gibbons have shown that human life existed near the summit long before the time of Saint Patrick, and the discovery of the ruins of an oratory there have added an exciting new dimension to the history of the mountain. From an archaeological point of view the importance of Croagh Patrick is only in its infancy.

Pilgrimages to Knock and Croagh Patrick and also to Lough Derg are gaining in momentum all the time despite the materialism of our age.

9

Politics and Elections

MINIMAL INTEREST

Politics was a subject which was seldom discussed within our family when I was very young, and while results were commented on when neighbours visited us after elections they were not a matter of high priority. My parents' interest in it appears to have been minimal. This was so despite the fact that there were four General Elections, a Referendum on the Constitution and two County Council elections held within a period of seven years in the thirties, and it was also a time when passions ran high because memories of the civil war were still fresh.

Before I knew the meaning of what they were saying I heard the bigger boys in school at playtime shout "Up Dev" and "Up Cosgrave." There were sometimes heated arguments between supporters of each side. These boys would simply be reflecting the views of their parents because even the oldest among them would be under fifteen years and they would have very little knowledge of the subject about which they were arguing.

For some reason still unknown to me, whenever there was a shouting or slagging match among the senior boys I joined the ranks of the Up Dev side. It may have been that it was easier to say Up Dev or perhaps I was more friendly with boys on that side. It certainly was not from either knowledge or conviction. Whenever I asked my parents who was Dev and who was Cosgrave they certainly did not go to any trouble with explanations. Perhaps I was rightly considered too young to understand. They made no comment when told that I was on the Dev side and had my allegiance been otherwise it is reasonable to assume that their response would have been similar.

The years went by, and while still in school I learned more and more about our country's centuries long struggle for Independence; the many uprisings; the 1916 rebellion and its aftermath, the civil war, the economic war which was then raging and the political parties. I remained on the Up Dev side, encouraged no doubt by the expressed views of our school master who was strongly republican although he canvassed openly at one election for Labour Party candidate, Dr. T. J. O'Connell because the latter was General Secretary of the Irish National Teachers Organisation. Practically all primary teachers were members of that trade union and James Murphy was no exception. The Labour Party was also republican and Dr. O'Connell was a native of our neighbouring parish of Bekan. Incidentally he was the only Labour T.D. ever elected in Mayo.

After leaving school I worked as a shop assistant in business houses in Claremorris, Ballyhaunis and Ballinasloe. Politics played no part in my life except that I attended a Fianna Fail by-election meeting in Ballyhaunis in 1945. Had it been a Fine Gael or a Clann na Talmhan meeting I might also have attended because neither of my two friends who accompanied me, Dom Moran and Tony Boyle were Fianna Fail supporters. However my unquestionable allegiance was to the Soldiers of Destiny. The meeting was presided over by Dan O'Rourke who was a T.D. for Roscommon at that time. Many years later I served with him as a member of the long defunct Western Health Institutions Board where I discovered that he was a man of the highest integrity who was blessed with a rare blend of compassion and wit. Incidentally while serving on that Board I first made the acquaintance of another Roscommon gentleman Paddy Concannon, who was a Fine Gael member representing Castlerea. We remained firm friends all through the intervening years and it was a pleasure to meet him from time to time and recall the friendships and deliberations of those halcyon days.

Long after leaving school I had discussions with my father from whom I learned that he, my mother and his parents had all supported the Treaty. They continued to support the Cumann na nGaedheal Party until the thirties when they changed their allegiance because of their opposition to the Blueshirt Movement. To a much lesser extent their altering course may also have been influenced by the entry in to politics in South Mayo of a neighbour from Cusslough, Micheál Ó Cléirigh. A cousin of the Prendergasts of Garryedmond he was a most popular and able T.D. and was probably the most gifted orator the Dáil had known. He resigned his Dáil seat in 1945 to become County Registrar for Dublin. He was uncle of Sean Calleary who became a colleague of mine on Mayo Co. Council and who, having been elected to the Dáil for East Mayo, was later appointed Minister of State at the Dept. of Foreign Affairs.

If my parents and grandparents in Garryedmond supported the Treaty, my mother's people, the McManus family, of Koilmore, were avowedly republican. Their house was a haven for the volunteers throughout the War of Independence and Civil War. On many occasions they got out of their beds in the middle of the nights so that men who were "on the run" could snatch a few hours sleep there in their stead. My father was a pacifist who always put his responsibility to his family first. At the time of the signing of the Treaty he had a wife, a child and two aging parents depending on him. So whatever about his nationalistic feelings he took no chances. Wishing to see an end to hostilities and believing that the Treaty was the best hope for peace, he supported it. In the same way he had no difficulty in changing his allegiance when he saw in the Blueshirt Movement an attempt to undermine the State and its lawfully elected Government.

JAMSIE MORRIS

However, my father's only active involvement in party politics was on the occasion when his first cousin and close friend, Jamsie Morris from Cloonfaughna, was a candidate for a seat on Mayo County Council. He cycled many miles covering a wide terrain canvassing relatives and acquaintances in an attempt to secure the seat for him. His efforts, together with those of many other friends bore fruit and Jamsie served with distinction on the Council until ill-health forced his retirement. His grandson Pat Guilfoyle with his wife Helen and their family reside today in Jamsie's old homestead.

Jamsie was a Cumann na nGaedheal stalwart who openly and sincerely espoused his political views. He was also a man of great integrity and compassion who, like most public representatives never spared himself in his efforts to improve the lot of the people he represented. He was a member of a commemoration committee which

KNOCK 1798 MEMORIAL
The names of the committee members inscribed on the side of the memorial are as follows:
Martin McLoughlin, Chairman; Patrick Beasty; James Morris;Patrick Lyons; Frank Burke; Edward Prendergast; Patrick Mulkeen; John Henaghan; Patrick Byrne and William J. Cunnane, Secretary

was formed in Knock in the centenary year of the 1798 Rebellion. Four years later a monument was erected in the centre of the village to honour the memory of the local heroes who played a noble part in that combat and Jamsie's name, together with those of his colleagues on the committee, is listed on the side of the memorial.

He died in 1934.

THE SPLIT

When the Split came after the Treaty the people of Garryedmond and surrounding areas were, as in the rest of the country, fairly evenly divided. The majority on each side kept their heads down and their views to themselves. Before the Split they were almost one hundred per cent Republican and supporters of Sinn Féin. The poignancy of the division has been amply recorded by many people who lived through it and who wrote about it. One of the side effects, as on such occasions is almost inevitable, was the emergence of a group of Republican sympathisers who became known as Bolshies. They were responsible for a number of bank raids and robberies, the proceeds of which went into their own pockets, and they brought little credit to the movement or the cause which they claimed to espouse.

While some people kept quiet there were others who were openly active and as their views and their actions were public knowledge I propose to recount some of their escapades as they were told to me. I do so particularly because practically all the people who lived through those stirring times have now passed on.

During all these years Mrs. Rose Kenny was a teacher in Koilmore school. She was a sister-in-law of my teacher of later years, James Murphy. With her family she lived in the teacher's residence and her two sons, Jack and Bill, were active in the Volunteers. The Kenny family were held in the highest esteem in the community, and no doubt their standing played a part in the large local support for Sinn Féin.

Jack held an important position with an oil company so his activities in the volunteers were of necessity somewhat limited. After he got married to Mary Grogan from Derryfad they went to live in a house in Kilbeg near Claremorris where some of their family were born. One of their sons, Billy, who qualified as a doctor was a brilliant footballer and a key member of the Mayo football team which won the Sam Maguire cup in 1950. Sadly for his wife and family and for Mayo football, Billy died at an early age.

After some years living in Kilbeg, Jack was transferred to Foynes where he played an important role in the development of the Air Terminal. Later he was transferred to Sligo where he remained until his retirement. He lived out his final years in Galway.

Bill Kenny, who remained an officer with the Republican forces after the Split, had many daring adventures to his credit. Among his exploits was a successful raid on The National Bank in Claremorris. The money garnered from this and other raids throughout the country was sent to Headquarters to purchase guns and ammunition and also to pay expenses. Within days of the raid a neighbour of ours was leaving the town in his horse drawn cart when he was approached by Bill who, handing him a suitcase, asked him to keep it in a safe place in his home. Some weeks afterwards Bill arrived and took away the case without revealing what it contained, but several years later he confirmed that it was part of the proceeds of the bank raid. Also involved in that raid were, among others, a local doctor and a lawyer which demonstrated that the movement attracted the most respected and influential people in the community who were involved because of the highest motives of patriotism, and their commitment to the freedom of their country.

Bill Kenny was an officer in the I.R.A. He was a "wanted man" and was therefore on the run. His home was raided on several nights but he was always lucky enough to avoid arrest. On some occasions he may well have been asleep in my mother's old home now owned by my cousin Kevin Johnston, which was only a few hundred yards from his own abode, or in some other friendly house.

He had a narrow escape once when the soldiers rapped on the door in the middle of the day. Getting no time to run out the back door he went into a bedroom upstairs and stood behind the door. The officer kept his mother and sister under cover in the kitchen while two of his men searched the house. They glanced into each room but miraculously did not look behind the doors. Had he been caught it is likely that he would have been shot because he was rightly regarded as a dangerous and effective opponent. As a result of this near miss he dug a large deep hole in the floor of the sitting room of the house from which he tunnelled an escape route underground leading into the back garden. He built up the side walls of the hole with concrete and placed the floor boards neatly over it. It was necessary for him to use this escape route many times during raids afterwards but at least he was able to stay in his own house in reasonable safety.

The house is now occupied by a young married couple and it has been modernised by them and is indeed picturesque. But for many years after the Kennys left, it was empty and falling into dereliction. During that time I often entered it with other boys through the open doors. The tunnel was closed but the hole in the sitting room floor was still there. While standing down in it we wondered what thoughts passed through his mind as the raiders pounded on the floor above him or as he escaped from them through the tunnel.

ATTEMPTED AMBUSH

One night during the Civil War there was a country house dance held in a townland adjoining Garryedmond. It happened to be on the night following the executions by the Free State forces of Liam Mellows, Joe McKelvey, Rory O'Connor and Dick Barrett. This may have been coincidental but local Republicans thought that there was more than a hint of celebration of the occasion involved. It also happened that they had information that a convoy of Free State lorries were to travel on the Claremorris/Ballyhaunis road in the pre-dawn hours of the following morning. So a group of volunteers arrived at the dance, armed and wearing masks. Accusing the people of the house and the dancers of celebrating the executions they smashed the lamps and delph and ordered the men who were present to go to Koilmore and cut a trench across the road at the corner near Walsh's house. One of those men, who was only a boy at the time, was appointed ganger. They did as directed, having first had to go around to various houses to collect pick axes, spades and shovels for the operation.

Digging the roads or rather cutting trenches across them was a regular feature of guerrilla warfare. The idea was to surprise the soldiers who would unsuspectingly drive into them and then find themselves immobilised. The armed volunteers would be waiting in hidden positions from which they would open fire. Because of the surprise element and their knowledge of the local terrain it meant that a small number of volunteers could defeat a superior number of better trained and better equipped soldiers. On that particular morning the soldiers failed to turn up so the road digging was in vain.

Another plan for ambushing was to cut down a roadside tree and ensure that it fell across the road. If one was growing in a suitable place this was an easier operation than digging up a road. There were no chain saws in those days and therefore felling had to be done by the slow and laborious use of a cross-cut. Depending on the size of the trunk, it could take between one and two hours to complete the task. The volunteers, who in the main were farmers, would meet in the morning to commence sawing and as timber was used for firewood few would suspect their real motive. They would make an incision about eighty to ninety per cent through the trunk and then leave it until shortly before the military were due to travel by, when they would cut the remainder. Waiting until the last moment to knock it ensured that if there were any spies or traitors about, they would not have time to pass on the information to the authorities and it would also cause minimum inconvenience to other road users.

THE RAID ON OUR HOUSE

Despite the total non-involvement in the physical sense of any of my father's family with either side in the Civil War, our house in Garryedmond was raided in the early hours one morning by the Free State forces. They were led by a man from Mayo Abbey district, and having expressed their belief that Republicans were being harboured there, they searched the house. Needless to say they found nobody nor any evidence to suggest that there was substance in their presumption. It was obvious that they had been given false or misguided information.

My parents could only guess at what caused the suspicion in the first place which led to the tip off. On the previous night one of their cows was due to calve in the byre at the rear of the house, and they made many trips out, using a lantern to light the way and to help them to see how the cow was progressing before the calf finally arrived. Although it was a backward place, the movement of the lantern could be seen for a long distance and it is possible that somebody, somewhere, spotted it and came to the wrong conclusion.

LIGHTER MOMENTS

Politics also provided lighter moments. At least they appear light now when we look back on them. There were two families living close to each other in Garryedmond one of whom strongly supported Fianna

Fáil while the other's support for Cumann na nGaedheal and later Fine Gael was equally intense. When an election was called, arguments started and the nearer it came to polling day the more heated they became until tempers were lost and discourse ceased completely. After a period of six months or so, which was the approximate time it took them to cool off, they would come around to bidding each other the time of day when meeting on the road. Within a further short time conversations would take place, as would helping each other out in chores whenever necessary. Eventually friendship was restored and visiting in each other's homes was resumed. But as stated earlier there were several elections in the thirties, some less than a year apart and it happened more than once that within weeks of the restoration of their friendship another election was called and the same old quarrel was re-ignited.

PUBLIC ELECTION MEETINGS

Before political debating on television became the prime method of communicating party views, public meetings outside Church gates after Sunday Masses and in the centre of towns on fair days were a feature of electioneering for all elections both national and local. The speaker stood on a fence or on a wall outside the Church and on a lorry or some other temporary platform in the towns.

The first election meeting which I witnessed was outside Brickens Church in the nineteen thirties. Speaking there were James Fitzgerald Kenny and Martin Nally who were both outgoing Cumann na nGaedheal T.D.s. The former, who for a short time had been Minister for Justice, was a senior counsel. He lived in a mansion in Clogher and was regarded as an aristocrat. It still seems strange to me that the humble and well nigh indigent people of south Mayo elected so many times this man with whom they had so little in common. Martin Nally, who lived in Claremorris, was on the other hand no intellectual, but a man of the people, loved by everybody in equal measure whether they were his political supporters or opponents. His speech that day in Brickens was devoted to telling his listeners of his efforts to have the River Robe drained and a promise that if re-elected he would have it drained prior to the next election again. He was heckled by two young fellows who reminded him that he had made the self-same promise at previous elections. I cannot remember Martin's reply but, as heckling was commonplace at such meetings, he would have had no difficulty in dealing with the situation. The young fellows could hardly have remembered much about what was promised at previous elections and what was obvious was that their parents were not supporters of Cumann na nGaedheal. At that time it could be taken as almost certain that all the people in a house supported the same party. Eventually the Robe was drained bringing great benefit to the farmers but depriving Martin of the main plank in his platform for future elections. His representations may have helped in getting the drainage accomplished but eaten bread is soon forgotten, and he lost his seat at the election following its completion.

When I was appointed a member of Claremorris Old Age Pensions Committee nearly a quarter of a century later, Martin was chairman of that body. We had many private discussions after the meetings and indeed many were the words of good advice he imparted to me. I entered politics myself at local level during that time, having been co-opted to Mayo County Council to replace the late John Gilligan. When contesting the next local election I too addressed many after Mass and Fair Day meetings but fortunately the days of heckling were over.

On my arrival to address some of those meetings it was somewhat frustrating for me to find Dalgan Lyons of Fine Gael there before me. He had a long and honourable career as a County Councillor, T.D., and Senator, and for close on three decades he held sway as the outstanding orator in Mayo, so it was not easy to follow him. But each time the receptiveness of the audience and our own close personal friendship enabled me to overcome the challenge. Dalgan and I travelled together to numerous meetings of community groups and we worked successfully on several schemes. He was a regular caller to my house in Kilbeg and I was grateful to have been able to visit him many times in his own home during his long and final illness when he received superb and unselfish care from his devoted wife.

EXIT AND ENTRY

At the time of my co-option to the County Council, two Castlebar men, Henry Kenny and Paddy Quinn were members. They had shared the glory as stars in Mayo's first All-Ireland winning team in 1936, and although on different sides of the political divide, their friendship remained steadfast. Henry, who had been a Fine Gael T.D. since 1954, was subsequently appointed a Parliamentary Secretary and his untimely death in 1975 spread a pall of sadness over the Irish political scene.

Early in 1967, Paddy Quinn suffered a mild heart attack. Local elections were approaching, and typical of his unselfish spirit, he immediately relinquished his Council seat, believing that for him to remain on would be unfair to the electorate and to his Party. The Fianna Fáil organisation in Castlebar area summoned a convention to select his successor who would be guaranteed the seat because of a gentleman's agreement that existed in the Council. The nominee of the Party which held a seat immediately before it became vacant, would not be opposed in a co-option. The convention selected an unknown – a young teacher named Padraig Flynn.

As I was the Party Whip at the time, it was my privilege to propose him at the next meeting. From his very first day in the Council Chamber the signs of future greatness were evident as the energy and ability within him were surging to exit and get things done. His outstanding achievements in the political arena caused no surprise to his colleagues, and his elevation to the position of E.U. Commissioner was richly deserved. The many honours that came his way did not alter his genial personality, or cause him to lose touch with his roots. He has remained the same Padraig Flynn through all his success, and it is reasonable to expect that he has yet to reach the zenith of his career.

THE ELECTION CAMPAIGN OF MALACHY FORDE

When the General Election was called in 1937, a prominent farmer and business man from Hollybrook named Malachy Forde decided to throw his hat in the ring as an Independent Farmers' Candidate. There was no farmers' party organisation in Mayo at that time, but he concentrated his efforts in trying to garner the rural vote.

He obviously had a great personal organisation or a huge number of friends assisting him in his campaign to judge by the publicity he got. On the road on each side of Koilmore school, and in several other places between Brickens and Claremorris a slogan appeared, painted in brilliant white on the smooth tar. It was in three lines and read as follows:

FARMERS
VOTE NO. 1.
FORDE

It was carefully painted and not just splashed or daubed so it had all the hallmarks of a professional job. The letters and figure were in block capitals and measured about two feet in depth. Considering the many times it appeared on this stretch of highway it is reasonable to assume that a similar onslaught took place on roads around Ballyhaunis, Knock, Hollymount, Ballinrobe and in all other areas where he hoped to collect votes.

Perhaps fear that Malachy Forde would be successful ran through the established political parties because that would automatically mean that one of their own would be a loser, or possibly it was just clever opportunism or fun, but some bright person or persons devised a prank in an attempt to put a halt to his gallop. It appears to be beyond question that the scheme was carried out by Fianna Fáil supporters.

One night about a week before the Election, practically all of the painted slogans showed a simple but subtle alteration. In identical brilliant white paint there was added to the name of Forde a final letter "V", and a hyphen was inserted between the "R" and the "D". It had taken the minimum of effort and of paint to place a new slogan before the electors reading "FARMERS VOTE NO. 1. FOR DEV". At that time Dev was in his heyday as leader of Fianna Fáil.

Forde's supporters later countered by painting new slogans in a slightly different lay-out which would be more difficult to alter. They put the "No. 1." immediately after the word "Forde" on the final line leaving no room for an additional "V". It now read 'FARMERS VOTE FORDE NO. 1." They did not show annoyance nor did they interfere with the signs that had been altered, although they had every right to feel aggrieved.

Despite his popularity, his ability and his organisation, Malachy Forde failed to reach Dáil Éireann in 1937 but he got a respectable nineteen hundred plus votes. It is unlikely that the interference with the slogans had any bearing on the result. Indeed it is difficult to know if such slogans have, or ever had much influence, but judging by the blitz at a Wicklow bye-election in 1995 the political parties have great faith in them still.

Malachy Forde did not contest any Dáil Election afterwards but instead concentrated his energy and talents on his extensive business. Founder and proprietor of Hollybrook Farm Produce Company he controlled its progressive ice cream manufacturing production from Church Street, Claremorris.

His decision to leave politics, although regrettable, was probably a wise one because of the enormous difficulties facing an Independent against the might of organised parties.

AN ELECTION THAT WAS DIFFERENT

An election that was different and which was enjoyed by candidates and electors alike took place in Claremorris in the fifties. There were five candidates in the field and while each tried hard to get elected the losers were almost as happy as the winner when it was over. Some losers were in fact better pleased. In one sense it was a contest where everybody involved was a winner and the more often people voted the better the Returning Officer liked it. There was no register of the electorate which was composed of everybody from the cradle to the grave who had sixpence to contribute.

It was part of the Festival of Claremorris and the election of "Mayor" was a vital factor in the festivities as well as being the most important element in fundraising. The total proceeds, which were substantial, went towards providing amenities for the town. Similar elections have become commonplace over the years but it was very new at that time and the first of its kind that I witnessed.

Thousands of tickets were printed and each bore the name of one candidate only. They were sold in every shop in the town and in any other available outlet and vendors had a stock bearing all candidates' names. The purchasers decided on the candidate they wished to support and accordingly bought a ticket or tickets bearing that name. The candidate in whose name the most tickets were purchased was declared elected.

All the contestants did extremely well but at the winning post Martin Cunniffe was away ahead. He proved himself to be an ideal Mayor. A delightful singer who generously shared his talent at all times, he was also a born showman, who, dressed in his mayoral robes, attended every function of the festival from the donkey derby in the racecourse to the thronged show dance in Isaac's. He made speeches and sang songs without having to be asked, drawing rapturous applause wherever he appeared.

Although Martin made the speeches and sang the songs the role of the "lady mayoress" was almost equal in importance, and combining glamour, dignity and originality provided a perfect balance to his act. On his every public appearance during those days the mayoress linked him as they mounted each platform, dressed in a flowing white gown and carrying a lighted cigarette held in the longest cigarette holder I ever saw. Having standing beside him a partner who displayed such charm and loyalty provided the mayor with great moral support.

The outstanding success of the part performed by the mayoress was all the more praiseworthy because it was played by a young lad who in due course became a leading business man in the town.

It was an election far removed from the intrigue, selfishness and back-stabbing of political contests but nonetheless it was an election.

A DUBLIN BYE ELECTION.

In the very early fifties a bye election took place in Dublin and in a very close finish the Fine Gael candidate emerged victorious. On the night the result was announced a very dear friend and neighbour of ours, Mike Comer, was in our house. He was very old at that time and he had been a weekly visitor to us for almost all of his long life. He had given his total allegiance to Fine Gael and its precursor Cumann na nGaedheal since the foundation of the State. It was long before the advent of television in Ireland and indeed before rural Ireland had electricity. We had an old battery radio and Mike was continually reminding my brother John not to forget to turn on the news at the appropriate time. He was interested only in the result of the bye election which he hoped and expected would be won by Fine Gael. Assisted by two young neighbouring girls, my brother had a loud speaker in the kitchen to which he rigged up a battery microphone from outside the house. Mike was engaged in conversation with my mother during this time and John went outside shortly before the news was due on the radio. The girls called for silence while they pretended to turn on the switch saying that it was news time. Then over the microphone came the words "The Fianna Fáil candidate won the bye election today with an overwhelming majority." John was continuing with sham details when Mike, flabbergasted with the news, ordered them to turn it off. They told him then that it was a joke but as he had no mind for airwaves or electronics or loud speakers, he refused to believe them until the genuine news came over some minutes later and gave a result which left him a far happier man.

Mike and his brother were well-to-do cattle dealers at an earlier period and although their trade was declining for many years it was the Economic War that finally put them out of business. As they blamed de Valera entirely for their misfortune, their antipathy towards him was perhaps understandable if somewhat naive. Mike could never comprehend how Irish farmers in the circumstances of the time not only voted for Dev and his Party but they did so in increasing numbers. I was sometimes fascinated at the pensive deliberations that on rare occasions took place between Mike and my father at election times. They just had discussions but never an argument. They were too close as friends for any type of altercation.

During the campaign on the referendum on the new Constitution my father asked Mike if he had given any consideration to its implications or provisions and the possibility that it might be in the country's best interests if it was enacted. "No! no! no! William," he replied, "Anything Dev is for, I have to be against it." Matters like deleting the oath of allegiance to the British monarch or electing our own President as Head of State cut no ice with Mike.

Although no relation whatsoever Mike Comer was my parents' closest, most trusted and most revered friend. He was older than my father but he outlived him by some years. He was a pal of my uncle, John Costello, with whom he sat in the same desk in Loughanemon school and in later years they went to dances and played football together. When my uncle went to America, never to return, Mike continued to visit in our house on a regular basis until his brief final illness. I once heard him say that he was coming to us for close on seventy years and he was fully aware of the welcome that always awaited him. One of his favourite sayings was that any man who lived to a reasonable old age was "once a man but twice a child." Although he himself lived to a great age his mind never deteriorated into second childhood but remained alert to the end.

10

The Emergency

WAR DECLARED

On September 3rd 1939 the British Prime Minister, Neville Chamberlain, in a wireless broadcast following the German invasion of Poland, announced that Britain was now at war with Germany.

For practically all of the next five years the news in the newspapers and over the radio was almost entirely related to the war situation. We were constantly reading or hearing of ships being torpedoed, cities bombed, battles fought and soldiers killed; the early successes of the Nazi forces, and then the invasion of France following the breaking of what had been believed to be the impregnable Maginot Line. Later we had the entry of Italy to the war on the German side and later still the entrance of America on the side of the Allies. Over the years we became as familiar with the pictures of Hitler, Mussolini, Daladier, Petain, Churchill, Stalin and Roosevelt as we are now with those of current world leaders. The question was often posed as to what could be found to report when the war would end. In order to conserve newsprint the newspapers were reduced to about six pages by Government order.

The following anecdote might help to illustrate how taken over we were by war news. Maloney Brothers had a high class victualling business in the main street of Claremorris and it is still a thriving business. There were three if not four of the brothers working and living on the premises. Originally they came from Knockatubber and I was at school with Martin and Jim, both of whom remained good friends of mine. They were all young at the time and none of them had yet married so it was a house where many people strolled at will into their kitchen or sitting room for a visit and to listen to the radio. Just down the street from them there lived a lovable character of late middle years who was nicknamed "Badly Bent". But far from being badly bent he was both erect and agile, and if the meaning which the word assumed in later years was then in fashion it certainly would not apply to him. Local legend had it that during his career as a jockey in his young days he was thrown from his mount in a steeplechase. Onlookers rushed to him and asked if he was seriously injured. "No", was his reply "but I'm badly bent", and thenceforth the name remained on him. Being almost stone deaf from an early age, when addressed he automatically put his two hands opened behind his ears to indicate his disability, and then by a combination of lip reading, intuition and possibly a little hearing he usually got the gist of what was said. On a Sunday afternoon he was alone in Maloney's kitchen trying to hear the radio which was on at full blast as Micheál O'Hehir was giving a running commentary on a football match. Apparently unsuccessful in his listening attempt he left the room but did not turn off the radio. On his way out a neighbouring man was entering and the latter asked him what was on the radio. He went through the formula of putting his hands behind his ears and then in response to the question answered "I think there was another ship scuttled". That phrase came over in so many news bulletins that he could be forgiven for assuming that he had heard it again.

LORD HAW HAW

The radio news was enlivened regularly by William Joyce who was better known as Lord Haw Haw and who made live broadcasts in English from Germany. Almost as essential to the Big Powers as winning battles on the field, the air or the sea was the winning of the propaganda war. Each side worried about what the negative effects might be on their own people and armies if they thought that they were losing, so it was important to keep up the pretence of constantly winning if at all possible. Haw Haw was a master propagandist on behalf of Germany and his job was not to maintain morale at home but rather to try to destroy it in enemy countries and especially in England. Night after night his distinctive voice could be heard..."Germany calling, Germany calling" and then going on to describe the latest war news always emphasising German gains. He had a huge listenership in Ireland and while some listened because they had a certain amount of sympathy with Germany or rather antipathy towards England, most people tuned in because of the wit and entertainment of his broadcasts.

The following somewhat poetic words from one of his broadcasts at the time France was being overrun by the German army are still fresh in my memory. "The gay-hearted men of France – we brought them to their knees weeping, the Pagan English – we brought them to their knees praying, and the squabbling quarrelling Irish – we united them all." William Joyce was born in New York but he lived in Ruttledge Terrace, Galway, throughout much of his youth. When the war was over he was captured and executed by the Allies. At the time of his broadcasts his Irish audience was unaware of the atrocities of Belsen, Auschwitz and Birkenau but Joyce could not be blamed for this heinousness because he played no part in it and was probably as unaware of it as were we. He was not born in England and therefore could scarcely be guilty of treason even if he had a British passport, so there was resentment at his execution around the world even among those who hated him. His daughter had his remains reinterred in the New Cemetery in Galway where they now repose, and for me there is no difficulty in breathing a silent prayer for his soul whenever I stand at his graveside.

CENSORSHIP

All news items broadcast by Radio Éireann and printed in our newspapers had to be passed by an official censor appointed by the Government. Thus it was ensured that nothing was published that could be used by one or other of the belligerents in their war efforts. Each side had spies planted about the country and all were trying to pick up any kind of information that might be of use to their respective Governments. Some spies were dropped from the air by parachutes but all were picked up by the gardaí within a short time and interned for the duration of the war.

They were not the only ones who were interned at that time. A number of young men who were known to be members of an illegal organisation and who were therefore regarded as a threat to the State spent most of the war years in The Curragh as "guests of the government."

Road signs indicating directions and distances to towns and villages were taken down, and those on buildings like schools or halls which would indicate the name of the area had to be removed or obliterated.

The importance of that decision can be appreciated when one considers how disadvantaged parachuted spies were when they landed in territory unknown to them. Although they had friends or contacts in some towns or villages it would be impossible to find them without asking directions from somebody. And everybody was alert when approached by a stranger and especially a foreigner looking for directions. The matter would be reported to the gardaí immediately and an arrest was a certainty.

Every letter entering the country was opened, read and censored when considered necessary. Recipients often found a line or two neatly cut out of their letters. In the same way correspondence addressed to people outside the country was censored.

There was a story in circulation at that time which may or may not be true, that a woman living in the West of Ireland when writing to her seasonal migrant husband in England mentioned that she intended to have the lower garden dug and prepared for sowing vegetables. In his reply he stated "For God's sake do not dig the lower garden as it is there the guns are hidden." However the garden was dug within a few days but the digging was done by the gardaí.

EMERGENCY POWERS LEGISLATION

The Emergency Powers Legislation gave the Government almost unlimited power to interfere with what had been rights of the people. But naturally when there was a threat to the State or when the common good demanded it, those rights ceased. So in order to ensure that enough food was grown to keep the population from going hungry it was decided to put under tillage a certain percentage of all the arable land in the country. Tillage inspectors were appointed nationwide whose job was to ensure that this particular directive was honoured.

The inspectors had very few problems in counties along the western seaboard because the farms were small, less than half the land was arable, and as mixed farming was the norm, by and large more than the quota was tilled. It was different in the midlands, south, and east where many farms were extensive and machinery and labour were scarce. Big farmers lost money when they were unable to save some of the crops. They also resented the intrusion of the State into their affairs so their welcome for the tillage inspectors was to say the least somewhat restrained. The Government also directed the owners of turbary to rent out banks of turf to people who required them. At first this interference was strongly resented although it was not resisted by the owners who in the main were farmers. However, they soon appreciated the substantial income from a source which they had never considered tapping and the scheme continued long after the Emergency Powers Legislation had ceased to operate.

RATIONING

A ration book was supplied to every person in the country, within which was a page of coupons for each item that was rationed. The consumer handed the book to the retailer who cut out the appropriate amount of coupons for the items supplied and then handed back the book. The retailer sent the coupons to the Department of Supplies at the end of each month, which in turn sent back a form of credit note to be used when ordering fresh supplies from wholesalers or manufacturers. Rationing ensured that every person in the country got a fair share of the goods available.

Cigarettes and such like non-essential goods were not included in ration books but they were very scarce. Manufacturers and wholesalers did their best to divide them fairly among their customers whom they supplied on the basis of their purchases in the year 1939 before any scarcity began. However some unscrupulous traders then sold them to complete strangers at black market prices.

As smoking and drinking often went hand in hand publicans tried to have a supply of cigarettes continually in stock. To achieve this they sometimes found it necessary to buy them from black marketeers but they sold them to their customers at the controlled price. A customer was defined as anybody who bought a drink on the premises. Therefore if one wanted to buy cigarettes in a pub it was necessary to order a bottle of stout or beer first and this usually merited five cigarettes. Beer and stout were among the very few items of which there was an abundance. As smoking is an addiction many teetotallers began to drink in order to get cigarettes.

Hardware merchants also attempted a rationing system of their own for items not included in the ration book. For example in one hardware shop there was a regulation that no single customer would get more than half a pound of wire nails at any one time. But some people found a way to circumvent this effort at fair distribution. A group of young people of whom three were of the same family entered one morning and each in turn asked for a pound of two-inch wire nails. Getting the stock answer "sorry but we can give only half a pound to each customer" they accepted the amounts and made the appropriate payments. During lunch time when different assistants were on duty each of the group entered again and went through the same procedure.

Scarcity and rationing did not mean that people were gloomy. There were a number of songs composed about The Emergency in general but in particular about rationing. The following are just two of the lines of a humourous ditty sung to the air of "Bless Them All":

> *"Bless deValera and Sean McEntee*
> *Bless Sean Lemass and his half ounce of tea."*

LIGHT FROM BRASSO

Candles were unprocurable for some of the war years. Paraffin oil was also very scarce and rural households at one stage were allotted only half a gallon per month. This would be less than one third of the amount required to keep a single-wick lamp lighting for a reasonable number of hours in Winter. When it was discovered that "Brasso" polish contained either paraffin oil or a similar substance people got a certain amount of light from putting a thin wick in through a small hole in the lid or cap of the tin and leaving out a tiny portion which they lit in the same way as if it was a lamp. I often did my school homework while using such a light. Needless to say all the Brasso in the shops was soon snapped up and it was not used for polishing brass.

As the war progressed the manufacturers of Brasso, finding it impossible to obtain the inflammable ingredient they had been using, substituted a noninflammable liquid which worked quite well for polishing. Hardware merchants however were unaware of the alteration and they ordered large consignments which were greedily purchased by their customers, who intended to use it as a replacement for the candle or oil lamp. Because the substitute element was useless for the provision of light, many tins of unused Brasso could be seen in rural homes long after the war was over.

NO JARS, NO JAM

A customer wishing to purchase a pot of marmalade or jam in a grocery shop was automatically asked "Have you got a jar?" The goods were supplied if the answer was in the affirmative but not otherwise. In most grocery shops a sign was prominently displayed announcing "No Jars, No Jam."

In similar fashion when customers required linseed oil or turpentine which were used for mixing and thinning paint, they were asked if they had brought a bottle. Usually they did not have one but most hardware merchants had a quantity of old bottles which had originally contained sauce, castor oil, vinegar and such like and were thus in a position to accommodate the customer, who as a token of gratitude often brought in a bag of old bottles on a later visit. Bottles were also collected by vagrants and offered to traders for a small monetary consideration.

SMUGGLING OF BACON

The only meat to fall into the scarce category was bacon. One reason was that some retailers sold it on the black market to smugglers who brought it across the Border where it fetched outlandish prices. As bacon was salt cured its shelf-life was considerably longer than that of fresh meat which was not viable for smuggling purposes.

Apart from that there was a scarcity of pigs in the country due in part to lack of feeding matter. Claremorris Bacon Company was the only sizable employer in the town apart from the smaller brush factory and the management found it impossible to get enough pigs for slaughter in order to keep their staff working. To their lasting credit instead of making many redundant they decided on various methods of diversification. Under their far-seeing and efficient manager, Jack O'Brien, a sawmill was set up within the factory grounds and trees were purchased throughout Connacht. A number of their employees were transferred to this new department. The Company also rented banks of turf and they sent other workers to cut, harvest and sell the finished product. Their biggest adventure was to establish a woollen mill within their building. This was a daring undertaking as nobody among them had any experience in this area. They took a chance and sent some employees on a crash course to a mill in England where they studied production methods after which machinery was purchased, and fortunately the venture was a great success.

THE ARRIVAL OF BORD NA MONA

The tranquillity of the nine hundred acre unit of largely undisturbed moorland in Garryedmond which had lain dormant for thousands of years was disrupted when Bord na Móna personnel moved in with their turf-cutting equipment during the Emergency. Known locally as Mary Anne Curley's bog (because she owned a large portion of it) and stretching from her house as far as Koilmore and Rannaghard it was a vast blanket of unspoilt heather-clad plain. It was a haven for wildlife

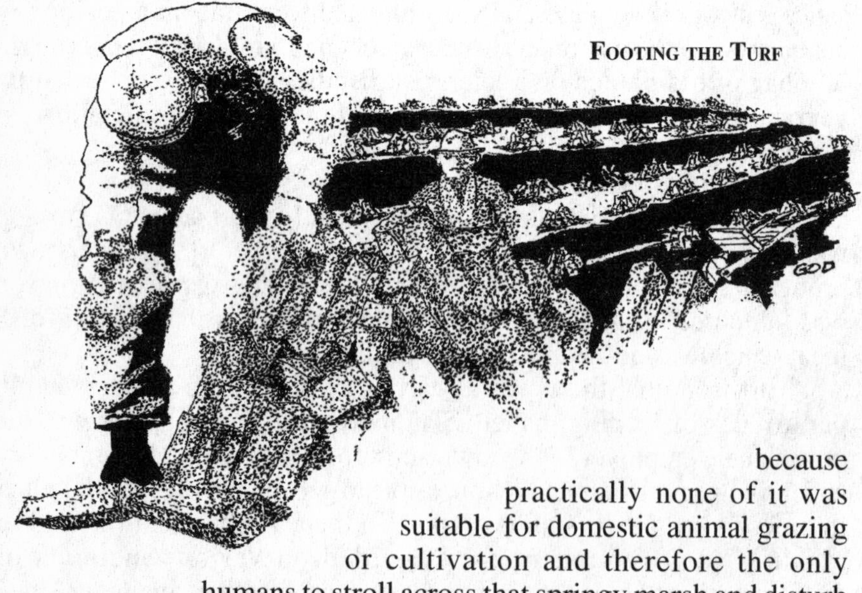

FOOTING THE TURF

because practically none of it was suitable for domestic animal grazing or cultivation and therefore the only humans to stroll across that springy marsh and disturb the customary quietude were the infrequent fowlers.

On arrival in Garryedmond the Board erected large Nissen huts which served as accommodation for the workers while they were partaking of their meals and sheltering from rain showers as well as providing storage space, which was their primary purpose. Within a short time they built a sand road through the bog which exited on to the main road near Koilmore crossroads where it still survives. Inspecting the new road was for a short time a novelty among locals and passers-by, but when this wore off it was used only by the employees until subsequently it also became a small-time lovers' walk in late Summer evenings.

The introduction of the machinery was a milestone in the evolution of turf cutting as up to that time the only implements used were the slane, the graip and the wheelbarrow. Under the new semi-automated method a number of men were engaged in digging the raw peat in rough chunks with spades, and throwing them into the well of each machine where they were intermixed, compressed and then forced out through tubes in sausage-like formation. A revolving blade then slit the product into lengths of about twelve inches and they were mechanically moved away from the source on a long, narrow conveyor belt. Four men, equipped with forks, were assigned to each machine to take the sods off the belt and spread them on the ground. Because of the compression there was very little moisture in them but they still needed a few days of reasonably good weather to dry out. When ready, the turf was gathered, ricked and later taken away in lorries to give heat in hospitals, hotels and private houses, and to provide energy in factories and driving power for trains. The machine-won product was much heavier and longer lasting than that which was produced by hand and it also provided more intense heat.

When compared with the modern appliance wherewith one operator on a machine digs, compresses and spreads the sods, the machinery of the forties was elementary, but at that time it was revolutionary.

Bord na Móna left the district after a number of years. During their sojourn in Garryedmond they gave good employment locally, harvested thousands of tons of turf and thereby made an important contribution towards the provision of heat and energy during that crucial time. After their departure the Land Commission took over most of the remaining virgin bog and distributed it in plots among applicants whom they considered suitable, and the cutaway portions were used for afforestation.

DEARTH AND DETERIORATION

As well as becoming scarce the quality of most goods deteriorated as the war progressed. Clothing, footwear, even shoe polish and almost all products came to be known as being of war grade quality. Flour and bread were by law only of the brown variety, as less of the wheat was wasted than in the white mixture. Strangely there was no scarcity of brown bread until the war was over and then it was rationed for a short while. The bad harvest of 1946 had a bearing on that situation.

New bicycles were quickly sold out and no new stocks became available for the remainder of the Emergency. Bicycle tyres were almost impossible to procure even on the black market. As always necessity is the mother of invention and before long the solid tyre made its appearance. This was composed of a large number of pieces of rubber cut into washers about three inches in circumference. A strand of wire ran through the centre of the washers which were tightly squeezed together. Both ends of the wire were knotted together thus forming a circle. It was made just long enough to fit tightly in to the rim of the wheel. As a result the bicycle became a real bone-shaker but people were prepared to put up with the discomfort, so pleased were they to have any form of transport.

MOTOR FUEL

By Government order private cars were taken off the road except where there was an absolute necessity for them. The reason was to ensure that as much as possible of the limited supply of petrol was available for essential services. These included ambulance missions, public transport, professional calls by doctors and clergy but each received only a ration. A less generous ration was allowed to proprietors of hackney cars and lorries. The former could be used only on essential business and on calls that were benevolent or humane like bringing patients to and from hospitals. Whenever a hackney car owner was caught driving people to football matches, coursing meetings or dances his licence was taken from him.

The amount of petrol allowed to lorry owners was so small as to be of little use to them. There was a mechanism called a gas producer invented at the time, and it enabled a truck to be driven on gas which was generated from charcoal while the vehicle was in motion, but only after the engine was started on petrol. Not having a mechanical mind, I have no idea of how it worked but I clearly remember seeing trucks with cylinders secured in front of the radiators. The gas producers were dirty and they caused so many problems that on occasions the cylinders were a camouflage while the truck was driven on black market petrol.

Diesel and electrically driven trains had not yet made their appearance and the prewar steam engines were all fired by coal. With the difficulty of procuring supplies of this fuel the railway authorities resorted to turf. Compared with coal the power was very weak, and as we listened to engines labour as they ascended the slight incline at Garryedmond we sometimes felt that the train would not make it. It always succeeded but often only after a great struggle.

INFLATION

It was during the war years that most of us heard for the first time the word "inflation." Every time that non-consumer goods were delivered to the shops they were dearer than the previous consignment. Traders who had a supply in stock altered the prices upwards in accordance with the current costs. This eventually became almost a daily exercise and it was quite legitimate. As goods became scarcer with each passing day there was no difficulty in selling all items at increased prices so the more inflation increased the more the traders profits were boosted.

But while business people did well there was no gain for the worker. In fact the Government introduced what was called a Stand Still Order, which prevented trade unions from seeking any general increase in workers' wages. This order was necessary in the battle against inflation but it helped employers to make even more money. In an attempt to counteract ill-effects the Government put a maximum retail price on food, some drinks and other selected goods like tobacco. Some unprincipled merchants charged their customers more than the controlled prices and for them the only deterrent to this practice was the fear of being caught out by Department Inspectors who were constantly touring the country spot-checking and who were liable to call at any time. Sometimes they posed as customers and on other occasions they just checked the price lists which it was obligatory to display. Fines for overcharging were extremely high.

BLACK MARKETEERS

More unscrupulous still were the traders who were involved in the black market of which there were two forms and one was as objectionable as the other. A trader bought scarce goods from a supplier either inside or outside the State at a cost far above the controlled retail price. He asked no questions as to how the supplier came by them because he did not care. His concern was to smuggle them or bring them covertly to premises of his own, preferably not his shop, where he sold them to anybody prepared to give him a good profit.

Like every emergency, even if there is strong suspicion that it will come, on arrival the preparation is never complete. The Department of Supplies did a magnificent job and probably could not have done better but nothing man-made is perfect. When the merchants sent in their coupons at the end of each month for essential rationed foods the Department recorded the number of customers each had and therefore knew the amount of rations required to cover them. But wholesalers and manufacturers continued to supply the merchants with quotas based on purchases made in 1938 or 1939. In most cases these were much higher than the amounts allowed for rations. As the trader could not sell more than the rations, he had to hold the balance on his premises and this surplus had to be available for inspection at all times. This may appear to be unfair but the merchant had the option of notifying the wholesaler to send him only the amount for which he had coupons. Many of them took chances and they sold the surplus in the black market. When caught, the fines for being unable to account for the excesses were equal to those for overcharging. It should be stressed that the people who indulged in black marketeering were comparatively few.

POSITIVE CONSEQUENCES

One positive consequence of the war was the spirit of co-operation which it engendered among the people. The County Councils did their part for the country by leasing out any land they possessed at a very nominal rent to townspeople as plots for sowing potatoes and vegetables. Some people took plots although they had no expertise in gardening but neighbours put whatever skills they had at their disposal. Turf banks were rented by others who had no idea of how to cut or save turf but local farmers helped them. A solicitor from Ballyhaunis had attended in his branch office in Claremorris every Monday for a number of years, while a dentist from the same town attended in his Claremorris surgery every Tuesday. As they could no longer use their private cars each had to employ a taxi. So they decided to travel together thereby halving their travel costs but one had to change his attendance day.

Most young men joined the Defence Forces or The Red Cross. Training took place on three or four nights each week, there were parades in various towns on Sundays and there were occasional manoeuvres with mock skirmishes with sections of the national army.

Ladies had their own branches of the Red Cross where their training in first aid was at least as intensive as that of the men and they also took part in parades.

DANGER OF INVASION

People rightly believed that the threats and indeed the possibility of invasion were very real but yet there was no panic. While the German bombing of Dublin and of Campile in County Wexford brought home to the public how real was the danger they still held their composure. It was a time when all our politicians left aside their petty squabblings and united behind the Government in their declared policy of neutrality. This unity at national level had a calming effect on the populace who had absolute trust in their leaders. When Belfast was bombed by the Germans, the Irish Government unhesitatingly sent fire brigades from Dublin to help the people there in whatever way possible. That sent a clear message to the Germans that whatever about the Border, Belfast was in Ireland.

When declaring the policy of neutrality de Valera was well aware of the fact that our small army with its meagre equipment would be unable to withstand an invasion. But he said at the time "If A invades us B will help us, and if B invades us A will help us." It was the only strategy available to him. Luckily we were not invaded by any of the belligerents. But Churchill in a most unworthy speech after the war revealed that on many occasions he was sorely tempted to do so. In his internationally acclaimed reply de Valera acknowledged the great temptation that must have been there but he thanked God and not Churchill for having spared us the horrors of the war.

11

Working in Co

THE CATTLE FAIR

Neighbouring farmers, who had cattle for sale, teamed together when driving their livestock to the fair. The minimum number of people required was three but this figure was usually exceeded in Garryedmond, at least until the pitfall of crossing the railway was surmounted. Many of the women folk went as far as the level crossing and then, having seen the men safely on their way, they returned home.

Every young rural boy from age ten upwards was brought to a fair at some stage. Some attended many, as indeed I did myself. For weeks beforehand the topic came up in conversation night after night as neighbouring farmers visited in our house. Old Moore's Almanac, which was a must in every rural home, was taken down from the shelf with monotonous regularity and from it were checked the dates of the coming monthly fairs to be held in Ballindine, Ballyhaunis, Kiltimagh, Balla, Hollymount and of course, Claremorris. Comments were made on the merits or otherwise of each. If buying, they were eager to go where stock most suited to their needs were likely to be on offer and when selling they were interested in going where the most buyers were likely to attend. Few farmers in our locality bought cattle other than calves and occasionally a cow. They reared the calves which they sold when two years old and if there was a suitable heifer among them she might be kept to become a cow. Anyway, despite all the perusal of Old Moore, they generally settled for the fairs in our own market town of Claremorris.

MY DEBUT

The fair was a very important occasion for the farmer as his standard of living depended mainly on his success there. When making my dêbut by attending one at the age of ten, my interest in it was not of a monetary nature for my understanding of economics would go little further than knowing how many sweets I would get for a penny. We rose at 4 a.m. on a cold October morning. We had three bullocks for sale and on the previous night they were moved for convenience to a small field by the roadside. My father, my brother and I waited at the gate until John Foy and Pat Lally, whom we had previously arranged to accompany, arrived and all the cattle were driven together down the road. One of the men walked in front to ensure that the animals were kept in close proximity while the other two remained behind them. We were well equipped with sticks and our job was to stand at byroads or at open gateways and direct the animals to remain on the main road. When these were successfully negotiated we jumped inside the roadside fences and ran on to the next such openings. Children, because of their agility, were more useful than adults for that assignment.

Getting to the fair early was important because the dealers commenced buying at about 5 a.m. One might have two or three railway wagons booked, and when he had purchased enough cattle to fill them he stopped buying for that day. Similarly if using a lorry, as soon as its carrying capacity was reached his requirement for that day ceased. So when each dealer had purchased his quota, it meant less demand for the remaining cattle and consequently lower prices. In October it was always quite dark at 5 a.m. and dealers and farmers alike carried torches, but despite the darkness and the hazard of lorries and cars driving through, there was seldom any kind of even a minor collision between animals and vehicles. Street lamps around the fairgreen gave a moderate amount of light but it was less than ample.

THE TANGLERS

Nearing the fairgreen every farmer was sure to be accosted by one of a group of men who offered to buy his stock. Having quoted his price, he would be bid an amount substantially less. The bids were sometimes derisory because these people were not genuine buyers but were known as tanglers who were retained for the morning by dealers. Each of them was hired to obstruct genuine buyers by engaging a farmer in tangling over prices until his employer, who was buying other cattle, was available to bid. It was an accepted tradition that while anybody was bidding or tangling no other buyer or tangler would interfere. It was very unfair to the seller but he could do nothing about it. Thankfully the cattle marts finished the tanglers.

When his employer arrived the tangler moved away to meet another farmer arriving with cattle suitable to his purpose. Some dealers were interested in two-year-olds, some in three-or-four-year-olds and others in springers or in milch-cows. After examining the cattle the dealer asked the farmer how much money he required for them. The latter automatically asked for a few pounds more than the amount for which he was prepared to sell them and in turn was offered a few pounds less than the dealer was prepared to pay. The offer was accompanied by the ritual of asking the vendor to hold out his hand which the dealer slapped with his own. A neighbour usually intervened and asked them to "split the difference" between what was asked and what was offered and normally this was the agreed final price. When the deal was made the cattle were driven into a nearby yard where the dealer was likely to have other animals which he had purchased earlier. This yard was at the rear of a public house where both parties met later at an agreed time when payment was made, and the vendor was expected to give back a few shillings for luck. This was known as "luck-penny." The buyer then bought drinks for all.

Sometimes the dealer asked the farmer to help him to bring the cattle to the railway station, where he arranged for the smaller ones to be transported to his own farm for fattening and the heavier ones conveyed to Dublin port for shipment to Britain or the Continent for immediate slaughter there.

TOLLS AND CUSTOMS

In 1885 the Ashbourne Act gave tenant farmers the right to ownership of land but, as they did with fishing and shooting rights, some landlords held on to the titles of tolls and customs in fairgreens and market places. The toll was a tax or a charge for the use of the venue while the custom was a charge on the goods sold and bought in the places. Originally vendor and purchaser were equally liable for charges but subsequently, and probably for convenience, the owners collected from purchasers only. The toll charges fell into disuse many years ago but the custom charges remained until the introduction of cattle marts. When the landlords died, their interests in the customs were included in their estates and passed on to their next of kin or to whoever they willed them if they did not have them transferred or assigned before their deaths. As time went by many of their successors sold their interests to various individuals. On fair days the owners of the custom rights employed people to man the various roads leading out from the town as well as the railway station, and they collected a small uniform fee from purchasers for every beast purchased. This was easy enough at the railway station as every beast railed was obviously purchased at the fair, but on the roads some drovers falsely declared that they were returning home with their own animals which they had failed to sell.

When the Bacon Factory opened about 1930 the pig fairs in Claremorris became obsolete as the factory accepted pigs directly from farmers. Although the farmers were the vendors, agreement was reached for the customs fee to be collected from them when they delivered their pigs to the factory for slaughter.

The fairgreen in Claremorris, within the deeds of which the tolls and customs of the town were incorporated, was purchased many years ago by a local businessman. After the advent of the cattle mart which heralded the demise of the fairs he sold it in sites for shops, private dwelling houses and the new Post Office. The corner on the Ballyhaunis road nearest Glynn's shop where the collector stood as he collected the custom is still occasionally referred to as "The Custom Gap."

THE STREET TRADERS

For youngsters, like myself at that time, the enjoyment of the fair commenced when we had finally disposed of the cattle. After a meal in a local café we were given a few shillings spending money. A stroll around the town ensured that we met other boys of our own age. There was a visit to the stands of the street traders who sold sweets, fruit and lemonade. There were other stands where household goods such as delph and haberdashery were sold. It was fascinating to watch the delph men bang plates on tea chests or make-shift counters without breaking them, and then throw them in the air and catch them with such dexterity as they descended. They acted thus to get the attention of passers by, while all the time they kept bellowing about the great value of everything they were offering for sale.

The most colourful and entertaining of all the street merchants were the Cheap Jacks. Those traders sold second-hand clothes which were always clean and pressed and looked like new. Their sales methods to say the least were unusual and could be described as Dutch auctions. A Cheap Jack would take from the rack a gents suit which he was prepared to sell for two pounds. At the top of his voice he would roar something like the following:

"Ladies and Gentlemen, I am offering the greatest bargain on earth. This fine suit is worth twenty pounds, but I am offering it to the first person who gives me ten pounds." He would pause for a moment as if he was expecting a rush of buyers. When naturally there was no offer he would continue:

"Then who will give me eight pounds?" He would pause again and then continue to ask for six, four and three pounds. When he finally came to two pounds, the tone of his voice clearly implied that he would go no lower. If nobody purchased he would leave the suit aside and take another one or an overcoat and go through the same procedure. Cheap Jacks were seldom without crowds of people around them, who seemed to be more interested in the entertainment than in the goods on offer.

Along with the practice among farmers and cattle dealers of bargaining over prices the antics of the Cheap Jacks may have played a part in creating similar performances in drapery and hardware shops, where most customers offered prices that were less than those marked on the goods. Fearing the loss of sale some shopkeepers acquiesced and in due course they developed their own strategy of counteraction. They simply marked on the goods a higher price than that for which they were prepared to sell them.

ENTERTAINERS

Also on the streets were musicians, ballad singers, jugglers, tumblers and three card trickers. All were trying to attract people and to get them to part with some of their money. Fortune tellers also graced fairs with their presence as occasionally did tinsmiths, selling their wares. Some of the latter group drank to excess on fair days and now and again ended the day fighting with each other. Some of those altercations were frightening to behold but for children it was still an added bonus to have witnessed a tinker fight.

Invariably very tired on arriving home in the late evening, yet we were prepared to wait up that night for whatever length of time we were allowed to listen to our visiting neighbours discuss in detail the prices they received; the prices other farmers got; the quality of beasts on offer and whether or not it was a good fair. Farmers were often economical with the truth when telling of the prices they received. They liked to add on a few pounds.

JUST A HICCUP

Generally speaking the public did not complain about the disturbance caused by fairs. Commercial travellers and other long distance road users found almost as much use for "Old Moore" as did the farmer, as it enabled them to arrange their schedules so as to avoid any town where a fair was in progress. The shopkeepers and especially the publicans made extra money from them and the farmers and cattle dealers needed a meeting place while the remainder of the people accepted that for them it was just a hiccup causing some inconvenience and disruption to everyday routine. Even the presence of animal excrement on the streets and on the shop floors where it fell from customers' boots did not take from the acceptance that this was a special day. Indeed the sweeping on to the streets of soiled sawdust which publican's had spread on their floors for the purpose of soakage, and washing down outer walls and footpaths was all part of the fair-day ritual, as was the removal of protective wooden gates when the day's business was over and the participants dispersed. The arrival of County Council workmen to clear up the grime and place it in carts for removal to the dump was the signal that the fair was finally over.

WORKING IN CO

Before the advent of the tractor the farmer tilled the soil by using a plough which was drawn by two horses. He steered the implement by holding a handle in each hand while at the same time another man walked beside him directing and controlling the horses with a pair of reins. Sometimes one man combined both jobs but it was much more difficult. Ploughing one acre of land was regarded as a good days work.

Small farmers owned only one horse each and as two were required to draw a plough they adopted what could be described as the "meitheal" system in miniature. Two neighbours agreed to work in company or in co-operation with each other. For economy of language this was described as "working in co" They either ploughed one man's requirements entirely and then went to the other, or they completed a portion for one and then a portion for the other if this was more suitable. If one man had five acres to plough while the other had only three there was no complaint from the one with the smaller amount. They were "working in co" and that covered all such eventualities.

If one man sold his horse and did not replace the animal he then had to employ a contractor to plough his land. In the meantime his partner had to look for a new co which could be very difficult and he might have had to travel a long distance to find somebody who was in a similar position. It sometimes took horses a while to get used to each other after a co changed or when one was sold and a new one purchased. It caused problems if they did not pull together but as most farmers were expert in training and handling their animals, with time and patience they overcame the difficuties. People sometimes parted company because of a dispute, but such an occurrence was extremely rare and it was much more usual for them to remain in co all their lives. Indeed those partnerships often went on to the second and third generation. When a man's credibility or respectability was under scrutiny as for example when matchmaking was in the offing it was a feather in his cap to be able to boast of having the same co for a good number of years.

I was about ten years old when my father sold his horse for economic reasons as he claimed that the equine animal ate more than three bullocks. He replaced him with a small pony that was not strong enough to plough but was capable of doing all the other farm chores of scuffling, harrowing, rolling and carting. Up to that time his co was our near neighbour Pat Lally. So my father had to pay a contractor to do his ploughing and Pat had to look for a new partner, but anyway he too sold his own horse within a few years. We also had a spraying machine and a harrow in joint ownership with Pat. No difficulty ever arose as regards both requiring those implements at the same time and it is fair to assume that a similar relationship existed among all joint owners in those days.

THRESHING THE CORN

In any activity on the farm in which it was difficult for one man to operate alone the co system existed. Naturally there was no necessity for this where there were grown up sons or a second man in a house, except in rare circumstances like the day of the threshing.

Although there were threshing machines in Ireland back in the twenties none of them made an appearance in Garryedmond until well into the thirties. Before that and indeed for many years in conjunction with it, corn was threshed by a flail. This was a hand-made two-stick implement. The larger stick which was called the "colpán" was approximately five feet long and was about as thick as a shovel handle. The other was about three feet long and had a radius of approximately one inch. The smaller stick was called a "buailteán." The end of one stick was tied loosely to one end of the other by a rope of straw or piece of twisted sack. In some parts of the country this tie was called a miodal. The man operating the flail held the colpán in his two hands while he swung the buailteán over his head and brought it down heavily but skilfully on the open sheaf of corn on the floor. In this way he beat or threshed the seed out of the straw. In the course of my youth I threshed many a sheaf of corn and I prided myself on my skill in so doing.

WINNOWING

When the seed was threshed out of the sheaf the mixture of grain and chaff remained on the floor and it was swept into a corner. The operation of separating the seed from the chaff was called winnowing. There were two methods of doing this and both were very simple. Where granaries were built over cow byres as most of them were, they contained two doors – one straight opposite the other. Except on a totally calm day, when both doors were opened a breeze blew through. The winnower used a riddle or sieve which was a round wooden hoop with a bottom of wire mesh the holes of which varied in size from a quarter inch square to almost half inch. He took up scoopfuls of the combined grain and chaff and standing in the centre between the doors he gently tipped it over. The grain being heavier fell to the floor and the chaff was blown out the open door. Chaff of course was totally useless.

Where this type of granary was not available the winnower had to go out to an open field where he used the same principle but he spread a sheet on the ground to collect the grain. The latter method had disadvantages. The seed and chaff mixture had to be conveyed to the field, and the separated grain brought in again to the store, and the winnower had to wait for a fine day and a fairly strong wind. Some of the wealthier farmers got winnowing machines in later times but so far as I know there was none in my native district and I have never seen one.

THE FIRST THRESHING MACHINE

The first threshing machine which I saw was a horse drawn apparatus owned by Bernard Trench from Brickens. My memory of the engine which was petrol driven is not clear. But as it was of the same principle as the later tractor driven machine it must have been detached from the mill. There was always difficulty in getting either type into gardens because the gate entrances which were built to accommodate nothing bigger than a horse and cart were too narrow for the much larger threshing mill. Pillars and stonewalls were often knocked either accidentally or on purpose to allow entry and rebuilt the following day. This procedure of knocking and rebuilding took place year after year because if entrances were widened, new gates would be required and many farmers could not afford them.

The day of the thresher brought out the best in the meitheal. Every farmer who was going to avail of it went to the haggards of about ten or twelve others to do his share of the work and they in turn came to his garden and did likewise. In what was almost a carnival atmosphere each man got down to his own specific job as soon as the thresher man got the engine going. The wide flaps on the roof were opened to make a platform, and on it knelt two men equipped with knives which were used for cutting the bands on the sheaves forked to them from the stacks of corn. A third man on the thresher top accepted the open sheaves which he fed into the mill within which, miraculously to my young mind, the seeds were separated from the straw and the chaff.

THRESHING MACHINE

The seeds came out in three openings to which empty sacks were attached and when full, they were carried to the granary, and stored there. Some of the seed was kept apart for sowing in the following Spring. The remainder was used during the year to feed fowl, calves and pigs. If there was a surplus, which was rare, it was sold in the markets.

As the seeds were brought to the granary the straw was exiting at the end of the threshing mill. This was taken away with forks and hoisted to a crew who were simultaneously building it into a large rick. It was used mainly as bedding for animals but some was also used as feeding.

During the threshing the chaff was continually blowing out from beneath the machine. The mill owner kept a ceaseless watching eye on all aspects of the operation.

There was not much competition among mill owners as there was plenty of work for all of them. But whoever was first to enter a townland at the commencement of the threshing season got all the work available there for that term. This was to change in our district when Johnny Keane from Cloontooa purchased a mill in 1950. He sometimes strayed to more distant places at the start of the season but everybody waited for him to return. He brought a new dimension to the enjoyment of threshing day, and his immense popularity remained undiminished for over forty years until his widely regretted death in 1995. I went to school with Johnny who was gifted with an ability to create unusual phrases, one of which I have never forgotten. While living in Garryedmond I was about to make what turned out to be an abortive attempt to become a bee-keeper and having told Johnny of my intention he replied "You must know a thing or three about them." It would of course, be usual to say "a thing or two" but ever since he said it to me I use the term myself quite often.

RATS IN THE STACKS

The presence of rats in the corn stacks was a torment scarcely any farmer escaped. But threshing day was doomsday for most of those pests. Young boys who accompanied their parents and who were armed with sticks and helped by dogs allowed few of them to survive.

It would take about three hours to thresh the corn of the average haggard and afterwards a hearty meal was served in the farmer's house. Here too, the meitheal was in operation as neighbouring women helped to prepare the meals. Normally the contents of three haggards would be threshed each day.

The torn up ground and the broken down walls and piers which the thresher left in its aftermath had to be repaired and the unsightly mess of chaff had to be cleared away. But despite those inconveniences the day of the thresher was one to which people looked forward, then enjoyed and finally remembered with nostalgia. It was a great exercise in co-operation and good neighbourliness.

THE HARVEST OF 1946

Late in the Summer of 1946, there was a prolonged period of wet weather which continued into the Autumn and there was grave fear that all grain crops would be lost. Dr. James Ryan was Minister for Agriculture and he appealed to business people, factory owners, financial institutions and to all engaged in non-farming work, to close down their premises on fine days to allow their employees to work at helping to save the harvest for farmers in their respective districts. The Government sent out army personnel and many civil servants were released from their duties so that they could join in the rescue operations.

The countrywide response to the appeal was beyond all expectations and it was estimated that over one hundred and twenty thousand volunteers went out from Dublin alone. Due to their efforts most of the harvest was saved.

I was working in Cogavin's hardware shop in Ballinasloe at that time. With all the male staff, I enlisted at the local Labour Exchange where crews were organised and despatched to various farms in the district. On the first day, six of us were packed into a car and driven to a farm about five miles from the town. In our group were four shop assistants, a post office clerk and a bank clerk.

None of my companions had worked in a corn field previously and they found the task of "taking out" oats and tying sheaves very strenuous. After a couple of hours they began to slow down, and then every few minutes they stood erect to relieve their aching backs. The farmer, who was sitting comfortably on a horse-drawn mowing machine became annoyed with their decreasing performance and he urged them to greater endeavour. "Come on lads; come on – it will be dark in a few hours," he called out over and over again.

Eventually his nagging irritated us. We were giving our best efforts voluntarily and without remuneration, and we felt that he should have shown more understanding. A message was quietly passed around by one of the group and then, without warning, we all walked off the field and up to the farmhouse where we had to wait over two hours for the car to come and collect us. The farmer and his workman had to continue working on their own.

Next morning, having assembled behind closed doors in Cogavin's shop, before proceeding to the Labour Exchange, we discussed the events of the previous day and wondered if the farmer reported us. We were determined not to return to him, regardless of what instructions were given in the Labour Exchange. On leaving the shop we met Paddy Kenny from Cloonfad. He was a school teacher who had about five acres of corn on his small farm. Teachers were on a prolonged strike at the time so he was free to devote all his time to the farm. He had just been to the Exchange, requesting help, but, not being a full-time farmer, he was put to the end of the queue.

We knew him as a customer in Cogavins, and in a flash our minds were made up. We ignored the Labour Exchange and crowding into his car, headed for Cloonfad, where for the next three days we helped in saving his harvest in a relaxed atmosphere, while enjoying the hospitality of the Kenny household and even the work in the fields.

WASHING THE SHEEP

Invariably we kept a small flock of sheep on our farm – seldom more than ten until lambs arrived and boosted the number for some months until they were sold. Each ewe usually gave birth to two lambs in Spring and later in the year its coat of wool was shorn off and sold to a wool merchant. We were fortunate in having in Claremorris area one of the country's largest and most reputable wool buyers in Luke Gilligan of Taugheen. Sheep breeders use the same procedure at present but one main difference is that they now use modern electric or battery operated shearing equipment, whereas during my youth sheep were shorn by a hand shears.

Before the shearing took place on what was regarded as a big day on the farm, almost comparing in importance with the day of the thresher or of bringing in the hay, the wool had to be washed while it was still on the sheep. Wool is greasy and can be quite dirty so the only place the sheep could be conveniently and efficiently washed was in a river or fast running stream. The nearest such place to our house was the rising River Robe near Luke Mooney's house which for a stretch formed the mearing between Garryedmond and Brickens. For this operation my father, my brother and I joined with Bally Prendergast who would have over forty sheep and we drove them to the river near Mooney's. It was an ideal setting perfectly suited to our purpose as the river bank sloped gently down to the water of which there was always a generous flow.

Although trespassing on his lands Luke Mooney always welcomed us. He was a man of generosity and this trait was also very evident in his daughters who for a long period had a sweet shop called "The Nook," in Donnybrook, Dublin, where in later years I often had the pleasure of calling on them.

Bally, who brought a change of clothes with him, waded a couple of feet into the river and my father caught and pushed each sheep down to him for washing. During this time my brother and I, assisted by the dogs, kept the remainder from rambling away. When all the ablutions were complete we walked them back to our respective homes and the shearing took place within a few days.

BURNING LIME

When Ned Byrne purchased his farm in Caraun he knew that much of the land was in poor condition due to lack of lime. This was somewhat ironic because beneath the soil in most of the arable land in the district is limestone. There was a disused lime kiln on every farm and the remnants of the one used by my forbears lie in the rear garden of our old home.

On Ned's farm the kiln was situated close to a lime stone quarry. He restored it and began preparation to burn enough lime to bring heart back into his land. The height of kilns varied but Ned's was about nine feet high and it was built into the side of a small hill. This made feeding it easy as the ingredients of turf and broken stones could be carted close to the edge of the top of it. The kiln was barrel shaped and fully open at the top while at ground level there was a tunnel or passage about twenty four inches high and some eighteen inches wide.

With the assistance of a workman he spent several days quarrying stones and drawing them near to the kiln. Using small lump hammers they spent many further days breaking those stones into small chips of about the size of golf balls. They had several tons of chips and quite an amount of turf in place before the burning was set in motion.

A layer of compressed straw to a height of about fifteen inches was placed on the floor of the kiln followed by a further fifteen inches of dry turf. Then a ten inch layer of chips was added. The straw, being very inflammable was to give the fire a start so there was no need for more than one layer, and it was set alight by placing red hot coals in the tunnel. When the fire was well under way they continued to fill the kiln to the top with every second layer of chips and turf. The emergence of thick smoke through the top signalled that it was operating successfully.

As the fire progressed the straw and the first layer of turf burned to ashes and the lower layer of chips burned into lime. As the mixture of ashes and lime fell to the floor the men drew it out through the tunnel with long handled shovels, and they placed it in a heap a short distance away. Meanwhile as the burning continued, the combined lime and ashes kept falling to the floor leaving an ever increasing space at the top. So they kept inserting chips and turf as required until all the chips were burned.

It took several hours of burning before the first shovelful of lime was extracted and it was at least a week before the last chip was thrown into the kiln. So night and day for that week the burning continued, and at least once each night the kiln had to be inspected and replenished with whatever chips and turf was necessary. The accumulated lime had also to be extracted.

The large heap of lime was most unsightly and messy but within a few weeks Ned and his workman had spread it over all the land where he deemed that it was required.

My father who had burned limestone in his own kiln long before I was born was helping Ned and the workman at the commencement, and because he was the only one present who had experience in this domain he was also directing operations. I was little more than ten years old at the time and I watched the whole performance with a great interest – indeed with fascination. Ned never used the kiln again and it was the first and only time in my life that I witnessed lime-burning in progress.

HUNTING

Snaring rabbits was an enjoyable and profitable pastime especially during the war years. There was great demand for rabbit meat from across the water and as the country was overrun by these little animals, capturing them brought welcome money to many people but especially to youngsters. Two firms in Claremorris were prepared to purchase unlimited quantities and they exported them unprocessed to Britain.

Rabbits always used the same track, or run, across fields and over fences and each family of them had its own burrow. They ate grass and the young growths of corn for sustenance, but the amount they consumed was minimal when compared with what was destroyed by tramping as they travelled over it and beat it into the ground. Not alone did they ravage crops, they also destroyed sod fences by their constant burrowing through them and under them.

Snares set on the runs were comprised of rabbit wire formed into a circle with a noose at one end. The other end was tied to a peg which was securely driven into the ground. When the rabbit ran through he was caught in the noose which tightened around his neck and choked him.

Usually snaring was done during the night so the hunters went out early in the mornings to pick up their quarry. They immediately slit the rabbits' underbellies and emptied out their guts which they threw on the ground. The offal was soon devoured by crows, magpies, seagulls and other predators. Had the hunters not gone out early to pick up the snared rabbits they would have found most of them torn apart by these marauders.

Rabbits grazed as near as possible to their homes which were the burrows in the sod fences, but when what was near was eaten, they had to move out further afield. It was not unusual to see them out from fifty to one hundred yards and the more numerous they became the scarcer was the grass and the bolder they seemed to get. When some of them sensed danger they did not instantly run for their burrows. They sat up and listened attentively but not before alerting their colleagues with a loud thud made by hitting the ground with one hind leg so strongly that it could be heard by the human ear a long distance off. They all sat up then and remained attentive and motionless until they heard or saw a further sign of danger. That could be a shot from a gun fired from behind a fence perhaps killing three or four of them, or the appearance of a person or a dog. The remainder would then scurry at great speed for the shelter of the burrow.

Instinct taught them not to fear any animal that posed no threat to them so they could be seen grazing almost side by side with farm animals like cattle, sheep and horses.

A YANK REMEMBERS

A returned Yank told me a story of an encounter he had as a small time rabbit catcher during his youth in Claremorris. The buyer's store was at the back of her shop in James Street in which she carried on a general business in hardware, grocery and bar. A public, but seldom used, laneway ran along by the gable of the premises and its adjoining yard at the rear. The yard was protected by a concrete wall about eight feet high and at the end of it was the rabbit store. He brought his rabbits into the shop where the elderly lady proprietress examined them and carefully counted them, after which she paid him four pence for each. She then told him to bring them through the shop and yard and to leave them in the store where there were hundreds of other carcasses. He went through the shop as he had often done before, but on this occasion when going along by the high wall, and out of her sight, instead of going to the store he threw the rabbits out over the wall where his pal was waiting in the laneway. He had to come back through the shop as the only other exit from the yard was a high, tight fitting galvanised gate which was constantly locked and he walked through empty handed and looking totally innocent. Some time later his pal entered and got paid again for the same rabbits. It was a big risk to take and if they were caught, the consequences, to say the least, would be less than desirable but the thrill of "getting away with it" was more important than the illicit and less than honest act of selling the same rabbits twice. It was a once off adventure as they decided not to press their luck by trying it again.

THE BURKE BROTHERS

A family of four brothers by the name of Burke from Clooncconnor made a profession of rabbit catching for many years and they were reputed to have become extremely wealthy from the business. They travelled en masse on their bicycles carrying their equipment which consisted of a box containing a ferret, several nets and a spade.

After the exits were covered with nets, the ferret – a small semi-tame animal of the weasel family – was dispatched into the burrows to frighten out the rabbits but he was first muzzled to prevent him from killing them. If he succeeded in killing one he would attempt to eat him and would not bother to chase others. Sometimes a long twine was tied to a ring placed around his neck so that if he remained too long inside he could be hauled out. When the rabbits saw, heard or smelled the ferret they ran in haste through the exits only to be caught in the nets. The brothers standing on each side of the fence grabbed and killed them and then replaced the nets over the mouths of the burrows.

When one fence was cleared of prey they moved on to the next and then to the next field until the oncoming dusk forced them to call it a day. After gathering up their kill and cleaning out their intestines they opened in one of each rabbit's hind legs a slit through which they pressed the other leg. They coupled them up and having placed them across the handlebars of their bicycles were a familiar sight on the nightly return journeys to Cloonconnor.

The Burkes were a very quiet and respected family. If occasionally it was necessary to do some slight damage to a fence when digging out a ferret they repaired it instantly. They never had to ask for permission to enter any lands as the farmers looked forward to their arrival.

A new rabbit disease called myxamatosis was artificially contrived abroad and was introduced to this country about 1953. It was highly contagious and appeared to be one hundred per cent fatal. Rabbits were to be seen along by the fences lying dead in their thousands with heads swollen and eyes bulging and the smell of their decaying carcasses polluted the air. Although they were the most inoffensive of animals and kept many a young lad in pocket money, no farmer shed any tear after them because of the havoc they wreaked on the crops. In recent years they have been slowly making a reappearance probably because a few became immune to the disease and survived. As they breed prolifically it will be only a short time until they are again a menace unless something is done to curb them.

Rabbits were far from being the only type of wild life hunted and killed either for sport or for monetary reward. Séamus Lally from Garryedmond owned two half-bred greyhounds at one stage and with other neighbouring lads I often accompanied him as we roamed over the local bogs in the hope of rising a hare. Hares were plentiful in our district at that time so we had many exciting hunts. Frequently they escaped but occasionally some succumbed to the superior strength and stamina of the dogs and were mercilessly killed.

A PROFESSIONAL FOWLER

A man named Martin English who lived alone in his house in Mayfield was a professional fowler. A quiet and well-liked person who found most of his prey around the lakes near Claremorris, he was unfailingly dressed in a manner suitable to his calling, wearing an unusual hat, waterproof clothes and wellingtons. A game-bag, often full, lay across one shoulder and a double-barrelled shotgun rested on his arm. There was no game merchant in the town but Martin had an abundance of regular customers there, who were at all times prepared to purchase for their own private use whatever wild-fowl had fallen to his marksmanship.

There were a number of sportsmen from Claremorris who on a regular basis patrolled our bogs, the most notable of whom was Paddy Keane from Mount Street and later from Kilbeg. He was always welcomed, because the local attitude was that there was plenty of game for everybody. He knew every fence, drain and swamp far better than the people who owned the property.

Game shooting is a great form of physical exercise because of the many miles walked over rough terrain in the course of a few hours. It also keeps the mind active because a fowler must be constantly on the alert for the sudden dart of a wild bird or animal from the cover of the heather or gorse. During the fifties I walked the bogs of Garryedmond, Caraun and Koilmore on countless occasions, gun at the ready, often alone, but sometimes accompanied by John Foy or other neighbouring lads. There was a plentiful supply of grouse, partridge, woodcock and snipe available at all times while pheasant and wild duck also made their appearances on our land as they do to this day. We were totally undiscriminating with regard to what we shot. Whatever bird rose we fired first and then looked to see what it was. Our dogs were neither bred nor trained for hunting but they did the job good enough for us. By chance we uncovered foxes too and they were automatic targets but our success in shooting them was very limited.

It is strange how one mellows with the years. I would not go so far as to support the extremists in anti-blood sports groups but at the same time I would not now, under any circumstances, shoot one of these creatures.

12

How Society was Structured

TOWN VERSUS COUNTRY

In my early years whatever wealth existed in provincial Ireland was to be found only in the main shopping streets of the towns and almost entirely among the business people. Professional people in private practice were also affluent but because of their small numbers they were less conspicuous. In the average small town there were no more than two doctors, two solicitors and one veterinary surgeon while one dentist serviced up to three towns. As chemists operated their own shops where the larger part of their incomes came from sales rather than from handling prescriptions they would be regarded as shopkeepers.

The shopkeepers dressed well at all times, their wives had fur coats, most of them owned cars and they took annual holidays. They sent their sons and daughters to college as the secondary schools were called at that time and to universities. From these students came the next generation of professional people – doctors, lawyers, dentists, teachers, civil servants and priests. It was regarded as the ultimate in achievement to have a priest in the family and most of them came from the homes of the wealthy.

Meanwhile the farmer struggled to make ends meet. If some had spare money it came in donations from the family in America or they got a legacy or had a trade or a part-time job on the side. It did not come from the toil on a small western farm nor was it contained in the weekly wage packets of the unskilled workers most of whom were from rural areas and still living in their parents' homes.

Inevitably the difference in income led to a difference in lifestyle resulting in social class distinction. It may be difficult to believe it now but there was a distinct air of superiority displayed by townies towards their country counterparts. The era when tuppence ha'penny looked down on tuppence was very real and perhaps strangely, the response from the rural dwellers was not one of resentment but of acceptance.

It should be added that away from the main shopping streets was also to be found real poverty among people of very low income, the unemployed and where there was long term illness. The farmer, although struggling, had his own home free of rent, his own produce by and large for the table, and to use an old saying "he trimmed his cloth according to the measure." The measure was often skimpy but at least he was never hungry. In common with the shopkeeper, if he died he left a tangible asset which was not available to the widow of a wage earner.

NO REGULAR INCOME

The main problems for the farmers were that they had no safe markets and no regular incomes. After World War One markets collapsed, the world economy was in chaos and Ireland did not escape the financial consequences. The situation continued throughout the twenties, reaching a climax with the Wall Street Crash. Before there was an opportunity to recover, the British, our main customers for agricultural produce, waged the Economic War against us when de Valera refused to continue the payment of annuities to them for our own land. The ensuing hardships were severe, calves were reputed to have been slaughtered at one stage because they were not worth rearing, and the government arranged for free beef to be given to the poor in the community. Dev had only completed a settlement with Chamberlain when World War Two was declared and that created further chaotic conditions in world production and trade.

Being a small island made exporting more difficult and having a sparse population did not help farmers in disposing of their produce. At various times throughout the year they sold corn, potatoes, turnips, cabbage plants and even sally rods at the markets, but their main source of income was from livestock and most of them had cattle for sale only once each year and that was in the month of October. The revenue received from the sale of sheep and pigs would only be supplemental. What the housewife got for eggs, butter and poultry was required for groceries and other day-to-day household expenses and for little emergencies such as replacements if the oven got cracked, the bucket leaked, the sweeping brush got burned, or a child had to be taken to the doctor. Luckily such expenses were only occasional because that income was irregular as both production and prices fluctuated. Egg production increased in the Springtime and then prices went down. With the approach of Winter production diminished and prices increased when the housewife had no eggs to sell. The availability of butter and poultry was also seasonal.

While the farmers were awaiting the proceeds from the October fair they had in the meantime to purchase seeds and fertilisers in the Spring and animal feed such as bran and pollard on a regular basis. Clothes and footwear were expensive items which had to be purchased whether or not they had the money. Many farmers could not afford to pay for these goods until they sold their cattle. They would not contemplate borrowing money in a bank in those days and indeed it was most unlikely that any bank manager would lend money to them. The only alternative was to purchase the goods on credit, so for a considerable period each year they were in the shopkeeper's debt. That situation automatically carried with it an element of serfdom which was both understandable and disagreeable.

EDUCATION AND THE LACK OF IT

Generations of farmers often gave the planting and harvesting of crops priority over the education of their sons and they kept some of them at home from school for days and even for weeks to assist them on the farms. In the days of the cane and the strap many boys were only too pleased and they were liable to be regarded by some of their peers as the lucky ones. Teachers seldom intervened and school attendance officers never seemed to cause much difficulty by impeding the decision of parents. The Department of Education at one stage made provision for farmers' sons to be absent for a number of days each year to assist on the farm.

Compulsory school attendance ceased at age fourteen and for many boys it could not come quickly enough. That was the end of their education for a number of them and it is possible that some never even read a newspaper afterwards. They continued working on the land until only one could remain and they then took unskilled jobs in factories, or as labourers with the County Council, Board of Works or with other farmers. Eventually many had to emigrate, mostly to England where they worked in factories and mines but mainly on the buildings. Most of them got married and raised families. Some founded their own contracting firms and progressed to becoming big employers and accumulating considerable wealth.

Of course some boys and practically all girls were anxious to learn and where there was no possibility of being sent to secondary schools they remained in primary schools with the blessing of their parents and teachers until they were fifteen or even sixteen years of age. From their ranks came those who got positions as Post Office Clerks, Rate and Rent Collectors and as gardaí. Some trained in hospitals as nurses and some were apprenticed to trades or to business.

APPRENTICESHIP

There was an axiom that there was more profit to be gained from a yard of a counter than from a farm of land and nobody was more aware of its truth than the struggling small farmer. While not aspiring towards exchanging places, he could do the next best thing by placing his sons or daughters as apprentices in shops and hope that one day they would emulate the shopkeepers who themselves had achieved their goal in this manner. Quite often the apprentice had no say whatsoever in the arrangement and some were brought in by their parents to be introduced to the shopkeeper for the first time on the morning of the commencement of their apprenticeship.

Whether in drapery, hardware, or grocery shops, apprentices spent three years learning the business. Although they had to work hard and do chores that could scarcely be part of the learning process no wages were paid to them. Where feasible they returned to their parents' homes at night but meals were provided on the premises during working hours. Where distance made the nightly return too difficult, accommodation was provided in the living quarters of the premises. In some business houses a fee was required before an apprentice was accepted. This applied mainly where full board was given but ostensibly it was a charge for being taught the business. Where girls were concerned it was quite the norm to see advertisements for apprentices stating that they would be required to do light housework instead of a fee. And it often transpired that more time was spent doing housework than learning the business.

DAY TO DAY WORK

The main work of shop assistants and apprentices was to serve customers but when not so engaged there were many other chores to claim their services. No matter how quiet the day, it was necessary to have one person available at all times to prevent theft as well as to be available to serve, and on those occasions apprentices were instructed to appear always busy. It would look bad if a customer, on entering a shop, found an assistant slouched over the counter or reading a newspaper in a secluded corner. So if only taking boxes from the shelves and putting them back again, the appearance of being busy gave the right impression. Practically all solid goods arrived in bulk at retail shops packed in large crates or boxes. Tea came in chests; flour, meal and sugar in large sacks and dried fruit in cartons. Apprentices and assistants spent much time weighing and packing these so that goods in paper bags containing standard weights could be handed out to customers on demand. Oils and other liquids were measured to order, nails and powders were weighed as required, while ropes, cables, leather and floor covering were cut to the requested lengths. Small tools and cutlery were kept in boxes, with one tied on the outside for display purposes and placed on shelves and taken down as required. Drapers and their assistants carried measuring tapes on their shoulders and pairs of scissors in their pockets. All were skilled in cutting cloth and in taking customers' measurements for suits and overcoats in an era when few purchased "off the peg" or readymade clothes. While there were shops in provincial towns where only boots and shoes were sold, most drapers also stocked them.

Parcels were wrapped in brown paper and tied with twine. Shop personnel were expert at breaking the twine after the knot was secure. This was done by twisting it around the index and middle fingers of one hand and when given a sharp tug with the other hand it broke quite easily.

THE LIVING-IN SYSTEM

It was a long road to achieving the ultimate ambition of most shop assistants which was to own their own business. On completing their apprenticeships most applied for paid positions in larger shops and usually in other towns. They would gain more experience and save as much money as possible. In due course if in good standing with a bank manager and with wholesalers, and if a suitable premises became available, they would rent it and branch out on their own. Some who were in no hurry preferred to continue for a number of years working in different houses and cities.

In some instances their personal freedom was hampered by what was known as "the living in system" which was current in the majority of provincial towns. In cities and in individual houses the staff were employed on an outdoor basis which meant that they got more wages and they made their own arrangements regarding board as was done in every other occupation.Under the "living in" system the shopkeeper provided food and lodgings on the premises and as far as the employee was concerned these conditions were not optional. As a rule keys were not provided for the entrance doors which were locked nightly at a regular time, normally at midnight. If employees wanted to go to a dance or stay out late for any other reason they had to request a key for that night. Otherwise, failure to return before midnight resulted in being locked out until the following morning. This often happened and all shop assistants had friends in the towns where they worked who were prepared to give them accommodation on such occasions.

A situation of far more serious proportions could arise when a shop assistant decided to get married. I have personally known a man who advised his employer of his impending marriage and he requested an alteration of conditions whereby the "living in" arrangement would be disregarded and higher wages paid in lieu of using the indoor accommodation. The employer's response was an instant dismissal. It was believed that he assumed the assistant could not afford to keep a wife on the wages that he was giving or would be prepared to give. A more likely reason was the disruption it would cause to the cosy and economical set-up of the system. The phrase "unfair dismissal" had not entered the vocabulary of the time and it is most unlikely that a copy of the encyclical of Pope Leo XIII "Rerum Novarum" had a place on the bookshelves of the employer. This encyclical was also known as "The Workers' Charter" and it upheld the right of workers to organise and fight for their rights and it defined their entitlement to a living wage.

A trade union catering for distributive workers and clerks was formed in 1901 but it was slow to get established in many small towns in the West. One of its basic aims was to abolish the living-in system. Despite its best endeavours and the inhuman nature of the practice it survived in many places until the nineteen fifties.

AN OLD PLOY

If a shop assistant asked for an increase in salary it was likely that his employer would refuse to give it on the grounds that he could not afford it or the assistant was not worth any more than he was already being paid. There were no standard rates of pay so the assistant would invoke an old and well recognised ploy to force the employer's hand. He would answer advertisements in the "situations vacant" columns of newspapers and sooner or later the offer of another job would come his way. Even if the pay was less he would say that it was more. When advised of the assistant's intention the shopkeeper, who would prefer to hold on to existing staff, invariably offered a similar salary.

The tactic was not unknown to the employer who in all probability had at some stage availed of it himself. However, if it was important for him to keep the assistant, he had no choice but to pay up. This was one of the few occasions when the assistant held the whip hand but he still could not afford to annoy his employer because the latter might not then give him a good character reference without which he would not be accepted in another job. Membership of trade unions which achieved standard rates of pay eliminated the necessity for that device. Trade unions fought hard over many decades to establish security of tenure, regular working hours, standard wages and uniform closing times. Almost as soon as success was achieved, they acquiesed in late night and Sunday opening and looked somewhat benignly at part-time employment. Strange things happen.

THE NEW SHOPKEEPER

When the shop assistant attained his aspiration and opened his own business in all probability he got married at the same time, and as might be expected, his wife was likely to have been a shop assistant also. It is undeniable that along the road they both endured some of the hardships of long hours, "living in" and meagre pay but this achievement made it all worthwhile. Extraordinary as it may seem, in many cases they then became as autocratic towards their new apprentices as their own employers had been towards themselves. It could possibly be reasoned in much the same vein as psychologists claim that people who were abused in childhood often turn out to be child abusers themselves when they reach maturity.

Anyway many of them developed the same traits as those who travelled the same road before them. Practically all of them made the few pounds and then dressed well, bought fur coats for their wives, provided themselves with cars and sent their families to college. They joined the local golf club and were invited into the Knights of Saint Columbanus. In keeping with their new-found status a respectable social distance was kept from their friends out the country although they naturally welcomed them as customers.

AN IMPORTANT ROLE

Having pinpointed the foregoing trends it must also be emphasised that the shopkeeper played a very important role in the community. In olden days when customers entered shops for even the smallest items they got personal service. They were advised about various qualities of goods and told which were most appropriate to particular needs. As stated earlier, credit was provided when it was required and money was lent to get over unexpected losses on the farm and in other emergencies. The shopkeeper arbitrated in disputes, helped to draw up wills and counselled those who came to him for advice. He was the main contributor to all things beneficial to the community from the building of churches and schools to sponsorship of agricultural shows. He charged no interest on money outstanding or lent, and no fee for any service.

Nowadays, in supermarkets and in department stores, goods prepacked in small quantities in the factories are stacked on shelves or placed on racks. The counter is a thing of the past. If customers are not familiar with the goods they wish to purchase they must read the directions on the packet. Clothes are all readymade and it is the customers' hard luck if none of the sizes on display fits. The employees at the check-outs would appear to be there merely to collect the money. Only in smaller family-run shops is personal service found today and regretfully these are getting fewer in number.

MESSENGER BOYS

The country woman carried home most of her parcels in a handbag placed across the handlebars of her bicycle and her husband brought the heavier and awkward items in a cart. The journey might be several miles. On the other hand the sophisticated townslady would not be seen to carry any parcel however small even for the shortest distance. If she had a maid she would send her to collect it. Otherwise the shopkeeper would have it delivered to her home by an apprentice or by a messenger boy.

Messenger boys were employed in many shops but especially in grocery and butcher shops. Delivering purchases to customers would not take up all their time but it would take a lot of it. They would also be engaged in collecting small parcels from the railway station, tidying up stores or the yard; preparing the return of empty crates to wholesalers and delivering by hand statements to customers who had purchased goods on credit.

The messenger boy was equipped with a specially designed bicycle which had a carrier over the front wheel which was of a much smaller size than the rear. On the panel between the two bars of the bicycle frame was painted the shopkeepers' name and business. This was a deft form of advertising and the more often the messenger was seen cycling through the town the better it portrayed the good business that was done in the shop. Many messenger boys had a distinctive habit of constantly whistling while cycling through the town on their delivery rounds. With some, it appeared to be an addiction but only while they were on the bicycles.

THEY WERE NOT ALONE

If business, professional and wealthy people looked down their noses at workers and people from the country they were not the only ones. Even shop assistants did likewise to a lesser degree but to a degree nonetheless. They would not associate with messenger boys, yard men or domestic servants, and indeed neither would farmers' sons and daughters. Strangely in prewar years when young Irish girls went to America a large percentage of them worked as domestic servants there. When they returned some years later usually with a large amount of money saved, there was great demand for them by would-be suitors including those who regarded themselves as upper class. The attraction may have been the money or it may have been the glamour surrounding "Yanks" but it is still inexplicable that the type of work they did in America was not acceptable when carried out in Ireland. Some County Council gangers would not eat their roadside lunches in the company of the labourers, gardaí officers would not drink in pubs frequented by gardaí, railway inspectors expected the porters to address them as "sir" while insurance inspectors hoped for a similar response from agents. And ironically in all cases the "superiors" were recruited or promoted from the ranks of the "lower".

THE INGREDIENTS OF CONVERSION

One of the main components in the alteration of social attitudes was education. Making secondary education available to all who were prepared to take advantage of it in the sixties transformed the whole outlook of Irish society. It gave young people confidence in themselves when they discovered that all could be academically equal regardless of their background or of their parents' wealth or penury. The provision of free transport to the schools was part of the scheme which created the biggest scholastic change in Ireland since the British government lifted the ban on education for Catholics in the nineteenth century. Donough O'Malley, take a bow!

E.E.C. MEMBERSHIP

Our entry to the E.E.C., now the E.U., also played a decisive role in altering attitudes mainly because of the wealth it brought to small and medium sized farmers. They became beneficiaries of wider markets for their produce and of many new grants for various aspects of farming. Within a short time their incomes were more secure and had increased beyond all expectation. No longer was it necessary to buy goods on credit from shopkeepers and they were courted by bank managers who offered them loans for modernisation and expansion.

To their credit, when their financial situations improved they did not hoard their new found wealth. Instead they concentrated on developing their farms, erecting modern outoffices, replacing outdated machinery and improving the breeding qualities of their livestock. They modernised their homes by installing up to date amenities and equipment, and where necessary building new dwellings. Farmers are now possessed of good education, often supplemented by intensive courses in agricultural colleges. Skilled in administration, employing accountants and other experts when necessary, they pay their taxes and run their farms in a business-like way. Bank managers, business and professional people are met on equal footing and they can hold their own in debating almost any subject. They take greater interest in the co-operative movement and participate more in its direction and management. Almost overnight farming became a specialised and sophisticated business and at last the farmer, who was always the backbone of our country, received the recognition that was his due, and he was paid for his work.

Whatever the shortcomings of E.U. membership may be, such as losing some of our sovereignty, the cost is small in comparison with the wealth it has brought to us all and especially to the farming community. It can scarcely be denied that if the farmer is doing well then so also is everybody else.

SOCIAL WELFARE

The wide range of benefits payable now to the less well-off in our society ensures that while some people are living in frugality they are not hungry unless it is their own fault. Recipients will not be able to take holidays in the sun on their social welfare incomes but at least they will not be deprived of the necessities of life. If some are imprudent in the manner in which they use this income the State can scarcely be blamed.

When gambling, alcohol addiction or managerial incompetence cause hardship in homes there is a wealth of voluntary organisations ready to help. Medical card holders have free medical services, free drugs and free hospitalisation. There are allowances for lone parents, deserted wives, prisoners' wives, disabled persons, carers, widows and widowers. In addition in certain circumstances pensioners have free electricity, free television licences, free telephone rental and free travel. Our social service benefits are probably the most generous in the world. Recipients are not beholden to anybody because of their legal and moral rights to those benefits, and when paying their way they can hold their heads as high as everybody else.

THE AGE OF CHIVALRY

When out walking accompanied by a lady the man always walked on the side of danger whether real or imaginary. On a footpath or out on a country road any hazard was assumed to be on the outside, and if they reached a river or canal bank along which their stroll continued he would walk on the side nearest the water because of the doubtless greater risk there.

On the morning of their wedding the groom was on the right of the bride. This is still the norm but present day protocol is not totally rigid as wedding photographs often reveal. The tradition is believed to date from the time when a warrior found it essential to have the freedom of his right hand to protect his bride with his sword if necessary. It would appear that all warriors and grooms were presumed to be right-handed.

When a married couple entered a Church for Mass or for any religious service the man walked down the aisle in front of his wife. He selected the seat and after genuflecting he conducted her in to it ahead of him. Men acted in a similar fashion, albeit without the genuflection, in a cinema, a train or a bus. Whenever a lady entered a room the men who were already there stood up as a token of respect and they did likewise when a lady rose to leave.

When a man met a woman outdoors he saluted her. If he was wearing a hat or a cap he raised it. Her response could be a smile, a nod or a verbal greeting. If she was accompanied by a man he returned the salute. Otherwise the only male to be saluted was a clergyman but like kissing a bishop's ring, this, and all forms of salutation other than verbal are now virtually abandoned.

Admission charges to dance halls, cinemas, sports, race meetings or any other form of entertainment were never paid by a girl if she was accompanied by her boyfriend or husband. Even if she was in employment or had an otherwise independent income it did not matter. The same custom applied when they went to a hotel or to a restaurant for a meal. Her income could be far greater than that of the man but convention ruled that it was his duty rather than his prerogative to pay all such charges.

Young women were never seen in public houses. The few middle-aged or elderly women who, when they met in town wanted to have "a treat" which might be only a cup of coffee, sneaked quietly into a snug. This was a discreetly placed small room off every bar where up to five or six people could have a private get together.

In most occupations it was obligatory on women to resign on getting married, so that other than one who was self-employed a married woman working outside her home was a rare phenomenon. It would be almost as exceptional now to hear of a woman giving up her job on marriage. Remaining in employment has given women more independence and it has also played a part in dispensing with the custom of the men paying for everything.

Up to recent times every woman assumed her husband's surname after her marriage but nowadays some continue to use their maiden names.

When introducing people of the same sex to each other it was conventional to introduce the younger to the older. On every occasion the man was introduced to the woman. Like most old forms of etiquette these courtesies have been generally discarded.

We have become very liberated over a comparatively short time. Common sense and pragmatism now prevail as all the old values continue to decline. However it is still pleasant to see men on rare occasions stand aside in a queue and allow a lady to pass, or offer their seats to women in overcrowded buses. Perhaps the age of chivalry is not fully gone yet.

13

The Changing Face of Claremorris

BÓTHAR GARBH

Up to the nineteen thirties there was only a small number of houses between the rear entrance to St. Colman's Church at Mount Street, Claremorris and the Convent gate. They were small structures, occupied in part by people who were considered rough and uncultured by the more refined members of the community. Because of the rough element it was called "Bóthar Garbh" which meant the rough road.

It is strange how things change. In due course this "rough" road became the most sought after area for building sites and the most fashionable place in which to live. When the whole area became populated by "reputable" people the name was changed to Convent Road.

The Convent of Mercy, after which the road is now named, holds a special place in the hearts of all Claremorris people because of the high standing of the nuns for close on two centuries, and the invaluable work they have done in the field of education. It has been lavishly extended but there has been but little interference with the original edifice, which is still a very imposing building. It was once the home of the infamous Denis Browne (Donncha na Rópa). Denis was the son of the second Earl of Altamont – one of the Westport Brownes who were probably Elizabethan Adventurers. He was M.P. for Mayo at the time of the 1798 Rebellion and for many years was also High Sheriff of the county. In his latter capacity he appeared to be a law unto himself, ruling with the proverbial rod of iron and annihilating his enemies by arbitrarily hanging them. The victims were almost always Catholics, including priests, who dared to cross his path, but at least one of the Protestant gentry also met his doom in the noose of Denis Browne's rope.

One of James Murphy's stories related to that victim, George Robert Fitzgerald from Turlough Park, Castlebar, under whose weight the overworked and well-worn rope broke as the executioner was attempting to hang him. Fitzgerald then demanded his freedom to which he was entitled under English law, but Browne refused it. A new rope was acquired but when the platform was removed, leaving the victim suspended in mid-air, the running knot in the loop got stuck, and try as they would, the noose would not tighten. Fitzgerald claimed that he was now surely entitled to freedom but

Claremount House / Convent

Browne would not relent. He ordered his servants to "soap the rope" and try again. On the third occasion the executioner succeeded.

In his book *History of Mayo*, J. F. Quinn has a version of the event somewhat different to that of James Murphy, but the basic facts are similar.

During my school days a story was in circulation that in Claremount House – by then the Convent of Mercy – one room was haunted by the restless spirit of Denis Browne and the locked door was never opened by the nuns. The door of another room was reputed to have had fresh blood splashed on it, and regardless of how often it was washed off, it appeared again shortly afterwards. Even after it was scraped and repainted, the blood reappeared so the door was taken down, burned and replaced by a new one. But the next morning the blood was there again so the door was removed altogether.

The foregoing are only legends which probably developed from the numerous times the evil deeds of Denis Browne were retold. He died circa 1811 and was buried in Westport.

James Browne, who was born in 1793 and died in 1854, was a grandson of Denis. He, also, became M.P. for Mayo and for a time lived in Claremount House. A later tenant there was the infamous Captain Boycott. Eventually the property was acquired by Rev. Richard McHale, Parish Priest of Claremorris, from whom the Sisters of Mercy obtained it.

The new Government, elected in 1932, made an immediate onslaught against slum dwellings in every city and town in the country and replaced them with new housing schemes. Grants to cover the costs were given to local councils with instructions to purchase land and move quickly with the building. At the end of Convent Road, in the townland of Lisnaboley on the Balla and Ardroe roads, Mayo County Council erected thirty eight new houses. The contractor was Jim Cunnane from Caraun who did a superb job in record time, and the houses were occupied as soon as they were complete. In due course the tenants purchased them, and as time passed, they extended and generally improved them. Other schemes have since been built in Boherduff and Luí na Gréine.

Across the road from the housing scheme at Ardroe, the Western Health Board built a new home for the elderly in the nineteen seventies. A modern building in pleasant surroundings, it answers the pressing need to make life as comfortable as possible for many people as they go through the third age.

TINKER STREET

Another street in the town which had a change of name is Courthouse Road. Like Bóthar Garbh it had rows of small one storey houses until well into the twentieth century and most local people over forty will remember some of them. They were occupied by, among others, a number of families who made a living from making saucepans, cans and other domestic articles from tin. They were in fact tinkers later to become known as tin smiths and the street accordingly was called Tinker Street. The last tin smith to occupy a premises there in which he carried out his trade was Pat Sweeney. He was a man of high standing in the community who conducted himself with dignity and carried on his trade in a business-like way, dealing only with hardware merchants.

The street eventually came to be called Courthouse Road because the old courthouse stood where the extensive premises of Patrick J. McEllin and Son, Solicitors, are now. The fairgreen was on the opposite side of the street. Like Convent Road the image of Courthouse Road changed rapidly and today it contains the new Post Office, Green Stores, several shops including a new shopping mall built by the late highly respected business man Joe Fagan, and the upmarket Casa Mia Guesthouse. The man who captained the Mayo football team to its first All-Ireland victory in 1936, Seamus O'Malley, made his home in Courthouse Road many years ago as did Joe Duggan who starred for Galway in the forties.

Entering Courthouse Road from D'Alton Street there was a very sharp corner. The house on this corner in which a drapery business was carried on was owned by Tommy Higgins before it was demolished for road widening. The previous occupiers were a couple by the name of Hession and all during my youth it was known as Hession's Corner. Because of the angle in which the house was built one corner protruded dangerously on to the road and at that edge, secured well into the ground was a jostle stone. The stone, which rose about twenty inches above the roadway where incidentally there was no footpath, prevented carts and later lorries and cars from going too close to and damaging the house. Of lesser consideration was the fact that it also gave a measure of protection to the passing vehicles. Some elderly male cyclists found another use for it. Gilligan's archway was a favourite place for parking bicycles during Mass time and when men were ready to mount their machines for the homeward journey they brought them to the jostle stone. By standing on the crest it was much easier to get astride before moving off on the slight upward incline.

Beyond Courthouse Road in the townland of Clare there is a hill on the farm now owned by Peter Delaney, which was a camping site of the British army of occupation. From this strategic place they lorded it over their subjects in the surrounding countryside. Some time after the Treaty was signed, the army was recalled to Britain and eventually the camps were dismantled and all saleable parts of them were sold. My father purchased a number of windows, which, after reducing in size, he installed in the dwelling house in Garryedmond, replacing the old smaller ones. Although deteriorating very fast they are still there. With my strong nationalistic outlook it is no boast for me to admit that the house in which I was born and reared contained such odious relics, but the truth is the truth.

MOP HILL AND OTHER ANCIENT NAMES

During my school days I often heard Lower James Street referred to as Mop Hill. Mop was believed to be a pun on the word "mob" as there had once been a boisterous element in this street also. The name remained long after the mob disappeared but for many decades it has been totally discarded.

Up to the thirties there were side-streets or lanes in the town which officially bore the following names: Paradise Alley, Fiddlers Lane, The Grove, The Lawn, The Prairie and Ball Alley Lane. My understanding is that they were centrally situated but it would appear that those names were not commonly used because despite my research I failed to discover their exact locations.

D'ALTON STREET AND THE DECLINE IN PROTESTANTISM

The Protestant Church in D'Alton Street now houses a branch of the County Library. This is a great facility for Claremorris and it is gratifying that such good use was made of the historic building which had fallen into a grave state of disrepair having been unused for decades. At a time when the religious divide in another part of our country was as deep as ever, it is refreshing to note that a spirit of toleration always existed in this district, and the decline of the Protestant population, necessitating the closing of the church, was regretted by all. In Crossboyne the Protestant Church also closed and the building is now derelict. Within the graveyard surrounding it lie the remains of Dr. Patrick Browne, distinguished author and botanist, whose name and achievements were unknown locally until the publication of his book *Flowers of Mayo* in 1995, by Castlebarman, Éamonn de Búrca. He was born in Woodstock in 1720, practised medicine in Jamaica for much of his life and on retirement returned to Mayo, settling near the family home at Claremorris where he spent the remaining twenty years of his life until his death in 1790. Although renowned outside Ireland for his writings he never got due recognition in his native country until the publication of the book, the manuscript of which was gathering dust for more than two hundred years. *Flowers of Mayo* is a source of unique botanical information and a masterpiece in craftsmanship. When the church was dismantled the Protestant Bishop of Tuam, Killala and Achonry presented its historic bell to the Dominican Fathers in Galway. It was re-erected at St. Mary's Church in The Claddagh about 1990 from where it peals regularly since.

The Protestant Ministers resided in The Rectory on the Knock road. Now known as Clare House it is owned and lived in by Liam Cosgrove. The incline which commences to rise near the entrance gate was known as The Minister's Hill. Up to recent years there was a lodge beside the gate and for a time it was occupied by a man of many parts who espoused deep religious views and was often heard reciting the Rosary publicly on the streets. He was a very colourful character who became equally famous as an agitator and as a failed contestant in both local and national elections.

Many other changes have taken place in D'Alton Street over the years. Where formerly derelict sites blighted the scene there are now fine buildings containing shops and offices. The old R.I.C. quarters had become the presbytery before my time and for more than fifty years housed many curates during their sojourn in the parish. Now in the possession of the Mercy Sisters it is in better condition than at any time in its history for it has been vastly renovated and the front garden is adorned with shrubs and flowers. The first boys' national school in the town was demolished in the thirties and replaced by shops while its successor in the same street is now the car showroom and display area of O'Brien Motors. But while the street lost two school buildings it gained a new swimming pool and a ball alley, both of which were built in the nineteen seventies.

McMAHON PARK

A large piece of ground opposite St. Colman's Funeral Home which once contained the town dump on the Brookhill/Mayfield road was purchased some years ago by the late Tom McMahon who was proprietor of Griffith's Garage. After his much regretted death his wife Marcella very generously donated to the town a large portion of the land to be used as a public park. Much work has been done to develop it and much remains to be done. It is hoped that within a reasonable time Claremorris will have a pleasure ground there that will be worthy of itself and worthy of Tom and Marcella McMahon.

THE WORKHOUSE

On the Ballindine road the oldest landmark is the now abandoned bacon factory which was built as a workhouse about the time of the famine. While it functioned as a workhouse in the time of my parents and their compeers I never heard them talk about it. But no doubt, like every other institution of its kind, many harrowing scenes took place within its walls. When famine and disease were rampant in Ireland they gave some amelioration, but the very name of workhouse has still a sound of horror in the ears of all Irish people, because the misery endured in them scarcely bears contemplating.

THE WEATHER STATION

Further out on the Ballindine road the Meteorological Station was erected in the thirties. It gave Claremorris great media exposure because there were only about six such stations in the country at that time and each was mentioned by name on daily weather forecasts over the radio.

THE BY-PASS AND SECTION 4

There have been changes, and all are for the better, in Claremorris in more recent years, and as we live in an evolving world they will continue. The biggest transformation on the horizon is the proposed by-pass. Generally speaking, as a society we resent change and some will regret the imminent implementation of this proposal. However progress cannot be held up indefinitely and the benefits will far outweigh the shortcomings.

Of great importance now is the fact that permission must be secured from the planning authorities for almost all new buildings. This should eliminate ribbon building, unsightly structures, narrow streets and dangerous corners in future. This can be only beneficial for everybody but I must confess to having piloted the first ever Section 4 proposal through Mayo Co. Council forcing the County Manager to reverse a decision refusing permission to a constituent to build a private house in Claremorris. In the succeeding years the use of Section 4 may have been abused occasionally but the success of my efforts in that case gratified me and I am satisfied that the final decision was justified.

NOT UNIQUE

With regard to housing and inhabitants, it should not be assumed that Claremorris was by any means unique. In truth it had far less of a rowdy or lazy element than most towns but it was more explicit in putting names on some streets. Those names were used occasionally when I was a child but they were only of historic interest because whatever original justification existed for the descriptions had long since vanished. In contrast there was a place in Ballyhaunis that survived until comparatively recent times which all residents longed to see disappear but it was known by the rather sophisticated and possibly appropriate name of "The Dardanelles." This place was a short, narrow and dark cul de sac with small, low hovels on each side. They were inhabited mainly by luckless people. It was overcrowded, sanitary conditions were deplorable and a stench reaching from it to the main street was sometimes overpowering. Apart from those living there, nobody entered except for grave or unavoidable reasons.

It got its name from the strait between European and Asian Turkey where, in World War One, a fierce battle was fought and many lives were lost. The comparison would appear to suggest that any outsider who entered it would be lucky to get out alive.

I never saw corner boys in Claremorris but I saw them in Swinford, Tuam, Ballinasloe and Salthill. The two latter places had what were known as "lazy walls" which were self descriptive. There was a sheen on the smooth worn stones that was the result of generations of lazy people having sat on them.

NOT A HISTORY

This synopsis is not to be regarded as an attempt to write even a small part of the history of Claremorris. There may well be important places or structures which do not get a mention in this book as well as notable events of which I am unaware or which do not come to mind. This is a simple summary of how one person has seen the changing face of the town over the second half of the twentieth century.

14

The Lure of the Land

SUBDIVISION OF HOLDINGS

In the nineteen fifties and towards the end of his reign as Taoiseach, Eamon de Valera was given to comparing the land situation with that which pertained in his own young days. "Nowadays" he was wont to say "the farmer has to plead with one of his sons to stay and take over the farm whereas in previous times he decided to whom he would give it." These were the days when Dev was advocating the idea of a dower house as an inducement to get a son to stay on the land. And in due course the idea came to fruition in many cases.

From the time of the famine and even before it, the love of the land was so deeply ingrained in the hearts of most people that any son would be glad to get it but that situation changed. There were occasions in bygone times when farmers could not make up their minds between two sons, so it was a common occurrence to keep both and divide the farm between them regardless of how small it was.

This was done in my mother's old home in Koilmore. Her grandfather, Michael McManus, divided the farm evenly between her father Jimmy and his brother Brian. The total amount of land was almost forty acres so each son received somewhat less than twenty acres. Both got married and they raised large families.

The old man while trying to be one hundred per cent fair in the division could scarcely have arranged a more awkward situation. He divided every field, no matter how small, in halves and they erected a sod fence through the centre of each. This left some of them mere gardens. In addition it meant that in regard to a few of them one had to trespass on the other as he went through part of the latter's field to get to his own. This could easily have created tension but luckily the two families lived in harmony. Many of their descendants, of whom I am one, are today living in Ireland. Some reside in the Koilmore locality while many others are dispersed around the globe. An obvious repercussion of the subdivision was the certainty that having to exist on half the amount of land owned by their father, both sons and their families had to endure a lower standard of living. In this case each son had almost twenty acres but many farmers with far less than that amount pursued a similar course.

A new house had to be provided for one son and this was supplied by converting into a bedroom the barn which adjoined the existing dwelling and then building on to it a kitchen, a hag and another bedroom.

In due course Brian's son Bernard inherited his father's half holding. But after emigrating to America he sold it to his cousin, so the old farm became one unit again. In the meantime one benefit resulted from the subdivision. The large Curran farm in Ballykinave which adjoined them was acquired by the Land Commission and a substantial addition was secured by the grandfather of the present owner. This would not have been obtained had the original farm been intact at the time. Kevin Johnston, a great, great grandson of Michael McManus is now the sole owner of the extended farm.

A ROMANTIC ROLE

Both houses were thatched but there is no trace of either now. At one time, each played a minor role in a little romantic history. When the old national school was situated at the crossroads in Koilmore close to where Martin Conway's residence now stands, a young John Kenny was appointed principal and he stayed at my mother's old home as a boarder. About the same time a young girl named Rose Waldron from Aghamore was appointed an assistant there, and she took up residence as a boarder in the house of Brian McManus. John Kenny and Rose Waldron did not need a matchmaker. Living in adjoining houses less than a quarter of a mile from the school meant that they walked together to and from work each day and this helped a romance to blossom. They got married in due course and they became the first occupants of the teachers' residence which was built in conjunction with the new school in 1893. This was the residence where all their family were born including their two sons Jack and Bill, both of whom played a heroic role in the fight for Irish freedom.

THE LAND COMMISSION

The subdividing of holdings might have answered a short term social desire but it created immense problems for the Irish Land Commission in later years, as well as for the families that had to live in miserable uneconomic conditions. Half holdings as they were called were sometimes divided again between another two sons in the next generation and all of this brought untold poverty in its wake. It was miraculous that the poverty did not cause starvation at a time when Social Welfare Benefits were unknown and there was very little outside employment available to supplement the meagre farm income.

When the Land Commission was established, its main function was to purchase land as it became available for sale in what were called Congested Areas. An area was recognised as congested if there was a number of holdings in it of less than twenty acres, which amount was regarded at the time as the minimum for a viable unit. This figure was later increased to forty five acres. Sometimes they acquired lands by compulsion if they were left vacant, were improperly utilised, or if the owner had emigrated or had left the area to work and live elsewhere.

As the Land Commission did not pay cash for lands which they acquired by compulsion, nobody wanted to sell to them. But there was no choice. No transfer of land could be finalised without their permission and if a sale was arranged with another party in a congested area they were likely to refuse sanction, and then take it over themselves. They paid the full market value in Land Bonds which gave a guaranteed annual yield over a specified period of years, at the end of which they were redeemable at par. But, as anybody who is familiar with dealing with bonds will appreciate, people may not get the par value if they surrender them. So holders were forced to hold on until the redemption date, or accept whatever amount of cash they were worth at any given time, and their value could fluctuate from day to day. As inflation was rampant during many of the years when the Land Commission was most active, bond holders generally were unhappy with their deal. What one hundred pounds would purchase in consumer goods when they received the bonds might purchase only one tenth of that by the date of redemption.

THE INSPECTORS

On the other side of the coin it was a blessing for the other local small farmers when the Land Commission acquired a farm in their midst, as each hoped to be allocated a few acres of it. An Inspector called to every household checking the ages and marital status of the occupants, enquiring if there was an heir apparent and examining the manner in which the existing farm was operated. They took all those matters into consideration when redistributing the lands. If a farmer was doing full time work outside of the farm from which more than fifty per cent of his income was derived, or if his land was covered with noxious weeds he was rejected as unsuitable for "an addition" as the supplementary allotment was called.

Redistribution of land was a long and laborious exercise for the Land Commission. Their Inspectors were strangers in a wary and anxious community which heretofore was close knit and charitable but was now suspicious of everybody – neighbour and inspector included. They all feared that a neighbour might do better than themselves in the redistribution.

They would try to conceal from the Inspector that they had a few fields set to a large farmer or to one from the next townland, or that it was on money sent to them from their family in America that they were living and not on what was produced on their farm. But other contenders were never slow to inform on them in the knowledge that as each farmer was deprived of "an addition" more land was available for themselves. So the Inspector, who was often offered cups of tea and glasses of whiskey, was kept extremely well informed but he had to sift for himself between the truth, the half truth and the downright falsehood. He had to make a judgment not alone on who deserved extra land from an equitable point of view, but who was likely to make the best use of it in the interest of the country, because the tax-payer was footing half of the not inconsiderable bill. The other half was to be recouped through the payment of additional land annuities levied on the allottees.

POLITICAL PULL

A particular anxiety was prevalent when some prospective allottees were active supporters of the political party or parties then in power. It was feared by some that the local T.D. or the Government of the day would direct the Land Commission to allocate more and better land to their own supporters. Some politicians, mainly of lower rank, encouraged this belief by promising their followers that they would secure additions for them. If the addition was received the politician was thanked, and if failure was registered, "sure there might always be a next time."

Indeed allocations were made from time to time which, like some referees' decisions on the football or hurling fields were difficult to comprehend, and people openly wondered if they were the result of political influence or bribes given to the Inspectors. Land Commission employees had every right to listen to representations but they were politically independent, and the vast majority were competent, honourable and impartial. If there were occasions when some of their members did not act in keeping with the high standards which people had the right to expect, they were few and far between.

MIGRATION TO THE EAST

At least as equal in importance as purchasing land in congested areas and dividing it among local small holders was the acquisition of large tracts in the Eastern part of the country, mainly in County Meath, and apportioning it in small but economic holdings among migrants from the West. If the farm acquired was in the region of five or six hundred acres it would accommodate from twelve to fifteen migrants giving them up to forty acres each. New houses and outoffices were built for them at Government expense.

After the departure of the migrants, the Land Commission had the job of distributing their holdings among the farmers who remained in the area. The amount of land vacated might not amount to more than from ten to fifteen acres each. If a dozen or thereabout left from two or three adjoining townlands the Land Commission in effect took over all the land in that area and re-arranged it as equitably as possible among the farmers remaining. Nobody was forced to migrate or to give up any land, or to accept any particular allocation. So the Inspector's task of trying to convince people that what he was proposing was in all their interests and that everybody was being offered a fair deal was a thankless one. Occasionally he was hampered in his efforts by a large farmer living some distance away and who was not entitled to an addition, but who had a field or two in among the small-holders. It was often diff-icult to persuade this type to part with those fields in return for a near similar amount adjacent to him. He had the advantage – which he used to squeeze an extra acre or two for himself. The Land Commission would want those fields to enable it to give each holder, including the large farmer, all his land in one piece. This was a point on which there was no disagreement as no farmer wanted to have a scattered holding in view of the extra work and expense involved in operating it.

When agreement was finally reached and the new holdings allotted, the occupants were given special grants to build new dwellings and outoffices if they were required, and needless to say they were required by practically all of them.

DISTRIBUTING CASTLEMACGARRETT LANDS

Of special interest in Claremorris area was the division of the lands in Castlemacgarrett. The total estate consisted of about two thousand acres. Six hundred acres were given to the Forestry Department, less than one hundred acres were included with the castle and a few acres were given to the G.A.A. for which they paid a nominal sum. This left somewhere over twelve hundred and fifty acres available for redistribution. Seven new holdings were created. Three of these were given to former herds who had been employed at the castle, and the other four were allotted to small farmers in lieu of their own uneconomic holdings which they surrendered. They had a choice of accepting new bungalows and farm buildings which the Land Commission proposed to build for them or alternatively they could themselves erect buildings to other designs towards which grants equal to the cost of the official structures were paid.

The remainder of the land was divided out in additions among small farmers in the district thereby bringing their holdings up to acceptable acreage. The task of carrying out this work was placed in the capable hands of their inspector, Ballina man Kevin Cowley, who planned and supervised the whole operation. It is a tribute to his integrity and ability that there was scarcely a murmur of dissent against any of his decisions.

SOCIAL UPHEAVAL

Migration was, quite naturally, a source of social upheaval for all concerned. However for those leaving, it eased the situation somewhat when a number left together and were settled in the same area in the East. A large group from Connemara were transferred to the Rath Cairn district in Meath over fifty years ago and they formed an Irish speaking community there which is still flourishing. For those who remained, the loss of their neighbours, friends and relatives was an occasion of sadness which bordered on that of a bereavement suffered on the death of somebody close. And it was not bereavement on the loss of one person, but a large fraction of the local community. At least when people emigrated to America, they left in ones or twos and the distress was more bearable for those left behind.

But all concerned had a choice to make. It was either to stay with a continuation of a life of poverty, or to leave in the hope of better things for their families and themselves in pastures new, while at the same time giving similar opportunities to those who remained.

When compared with what our ancestors of some generations back had to endure when they left their homes in the hope of conquering the new world, the cause for anxiety was minuscule. The former travelled on the raging seas in ill-equipped ships and faced the great unknown. In contrast the migrants were about to settle comfortably in new houses in their own country, and among fellow Irish men and women, most of whom welcomed them with hospitality and generosity.

HOLY POVERTY

Speeches were often made by politicians (but only when they were in opposition) and sermons were preached by clergy, including bishops, decrying the migration and lamenting the population denudation of their parishes. Of course upsetting the existing tradition was regrettable but none of these critics suggested an alternative. They just continued to use the hackneyed phrase "Something will have to be done for the small farmer." But generally speaking, they objected to dole payments because they regarded them as demeaning and they did nothing, and admittedly could scarcely do anything to bring employment to their districts. Yet when something was being done to bring relief to the situation they objected. When a bishop berated the late Micheál Ó Móráin, who as Minister for Lands had presided over a fair measure of migration he replied "At least I am helping to raise the standard of living for those people. All you offer is criticism while you are prepared to condemn your flock to a continuation of life in holy poverty." He put emphasis on the word "holy."

Most of the critics were themselves born in rural Ireland which they left for a better life in the towns and cities. They would not return but they expected others to remain and accept the deprivation which then existed and which they themselves had no difficulty in forsaking.

Without exception the migrants settled well in their places of adoption and they prospered. They showed commendable courage in accepting the rather trying change when it was offered to them. If their ancestors had shown the same kind of grit and foresight, and had made equally painful decisions when subdividing their holdings, a lot of unnecessary future sadness and turmoil would have been avoided.

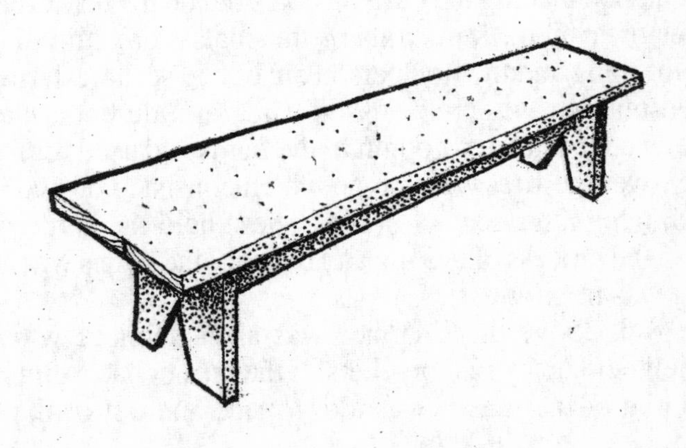

15

Unhurried Country Life

WITHIN THE KITCHEN

The open hearth fire was the focus point in the kitchen. Each night the family and their friends sat around it in a semi-circle which widened as each additional visitor entered. The fire was never extinguished because even on the warmest Summer day it was needed to boil water for the tea and it provided the housewife's only means of cooking. And when the visitors exited at night and the family retired to their beds, the last person leaving the kitchen, raked it. This simple operation entailed placing the burning coals flat on the hearth and gently piling ashes over them. Remnants of the coals were still alive on the following morning and the first person out of bed set a fresh fire aflame. The burned-out ash was first pushed aside and dumped later in the ashpit. In due course it was brought to the fields and used for fertilising.

Directly over the fire was a crane which consisted of two iron rails from which hung a number of hooks. These held the kettle while the water was in the process of boiling and the pots and ovens when cooking and baking was in progress.

On the wall above the fireplace was a mantelpiece which was a wooden shelf held up by two brackets. If the farmer had a gun it usually nestled on one of them as it was a dry place and out of the reach of children.

Small harmless insects called crickets hovered around the hearth after the fire was raked and the light put out. They could be heard chirping for a short time and then, like the people, they apparently went to sleep too. Superstitious folk believed that the little creatures brought good luck and when leaving an old house some were known to bring the crickets to their new abode.

BESIDE THE FIRE

A form (pronounced fur-um) was a long plain seat comprising basically of one well-planed board about one inch in thickness and about ten inches wide. It could be from five to seven feet long and it rested on two wooden stands or supports to which it was firmly screwed. The supports were about twelve inches in from the ends and it stood the height of the average chair. Grooved boards sometimes ran along the edges of the seat but they served no purpose other than adornment. Forms were usually scrubbed clean and seldom painted.

We had two short forms fixed to the wall in our entrance hall and they were used for leaving buckets of water upon them but the more usual and obvious purpose was to seat people. It was a simple piece of furniture which most handymen could make. If only two people were sitting on it, one at each end, and if either rose without warning, the weight of the other would cause it to heave up and topple him to the floor unless he was very agile. That was about the only defect in what was a useful seat that could be moved about easily. They were often lent to neighbours for dances and weddings.

At least one home-made stool could be seen under every kitchen table during the day, and if the people sitting around the fire at night had occupied all the other modes of seating it was used as an additional seat. It had a smoothly-planed round seat into which three short legs were mortised. Some had wooden rails tenoned into the legs for added strength but if the stool was properly made they were unnecessary. The reason it had only three legs compared with the modern four legged kitchen or bar stool was not to save timber or time when making it, but because many floors were flagged and therefore uneven, it was easier to balance the three legged variety. A four legged stool on an uneven floor would be decidedly uncomfortable. Stools were also used when hand-milking cows both in the byre and in the field.

Almost every country house boasted of a settle-bed when large families were the norm. It was a large oblong wooden seat during the day which at night could be opened out and four people could comfortably sleep in it. It was a heavy piece of furniture which was left in a permanent position in the kitchen. Unlike the stool or the form it took a skilled carpenter to make one. There were few to be seen during my young days and, as the average size of families became smaller and when people built new houses and installed modern furniture, the settle-beds disappeared.

Half doors were, if I may use a pun, on the way out when I was growing up. Old photographs of our own house, which is still standing, show a half door but I never saw it. However there were still a few of them about but as houses became modernised and when new doors were installed at the time of Stations the old half doors were not replaced. Many old people lamented their passing as they had served useful functions in their time. They kept the hens and other domestic fowl from entering the kitchen while they allowed in the fresh air and the sunlight. Pipe-smoking elderly men were often to be seen leaning on them and relaxing as they watched for any neighbour to pass with whom they could snatch a morsel of conversation. They provided material for writers of songs and stories for decades and they served as protection for young children by preventing them from walking or creeping outdoors.

Similarly fire guards protected young children from the dangers of the open hearth fires. These were strong wire meshes which were held firmly by hooks embedded in the wall on each side of the hearth.

The dresser was the showpiece of the kitchen. It was about four feet in length and stood almost the height of the sidewall. The lower portion was a large shelved press about thirty inches high, twenty four inches deep and with two doors opening outwards. Within the presses the housewife kept bread, crocks of milk, butter, jam and meat. Sometimes pans and saucepans were also stored there.

The upper portion, which reached almost to the lowest board of the ceiling, consisted of open shelves on which were placed the delph in everyday use, including cups, saucers, plates, egg cups, dishes and teapots. A small space was left for the alarm clock. The china tea set was never placed on the dresser. As it was highly valued and handed down from one generation to the next, it held an honoured place safely stacked in the chiffonier which was kept in the parlour where one existed, and otherwise in the principal bedroom.

Holy pictures adorned the walls and a Sacred Heart lamp was perpetually lighting beneath the appropriate picture. Even when the supply of paraffin oil was severely curtailed during the war years this lamp had first call on what was available.

The table and chairs differed little from those in use at present except that they were always made of timber and the same applies to the twig or sweeping brush, but in bygone days to ensure their longevity many housewives substituted homemade heather brooms for sweeping in hot ashes which fell beyond the hearth.

The running of the kitchen was the sole prerogative of the housewife. Within this room she did practically all of her work and controlled the activities of the home. There she made the bread, churned the milk and cooked the meals. She washed the clothes in a large galvanised bath by scrubbing them with her bare hands against a washboard and using hot water and soap. She ironed the clothes with a smoothing iron which was an appliance of much the same shape as the modern electric iron. To generate heat, the bottom was placed against the burning coals on the fire. When it had absorbed as much heat as possible, she cleaned it with a light rub of a dry cloth and continued to iron until it went cool. She then replaced it against the coals and waited for it to reheat. If there was a second iron it would be left heating while the first was in use and ironing could continue nonstop. That was the only type of iron used in our house and we still have one which serves as a reminder of the past. There were other types used and the most popular was the box iron, which contained a removable brick which could be heated in the fire.

It was also in the kitchen that the housewife entertained her callers including the casual visitor, the postman, the gárda taking the census, the wrenboys, the pedlar and the vagrant.

CHIMNEY CLEANING

During the thirties and forties the chimney sweep was a familiar sight as he travelled on foot through the countryside in search of work at his chosen trade. On his shoulder lay a bundle of rods which, when in use, were screwed into each other. Attached to one was a circular brush-head and to another a triangular steel scraper. Similar type rods are still in use for chimney cleaning and in the clearance of clogged sewerage pipes.

If he secured an engagement on entering a house, there was an immediate flurry as the housewife got a number of canvas sacks which she hurriedly sewed together with a packing needle and twine. The fire was taken out and the sewn canvas was draped from the mantlepiece in an attempt to keep the soot within its fold. The sweep first scraped and then brushed the chimney walls right to the top, bringing the soot down to the hearth. Then having completed his part of the job, he unscrewed the rods and, collecting his fee, continued on his way.

Before the canvas was taken down the heap of soot was allowed to settle and then it was gently filled into a bucket and dumped in the ashpit or used in the garden. Despite the covering, some of the soot escaped and settled on the walls, ceiling and floor leaving a nasty odour about. It took several hours and many dustings and sweepings before the kitchen was soot-free again.

Sometimes a farmer did not wait for the arrival of the sweep to have the chimney cleaned. He got a furze bush and compressed it to the size of the narrowest point of the inside of the funnel. Then climbing on to the roof and bringing with him a long rope he let one end of it drop to the floor while holding the other end himself. A helper, waiting at the hearth, tied the centre of the rope around the bush. The man on the roof pulled the rope upwards until the bush reached him and then it was pulled down again. The see-saw continued until the chimney was cleaned.

Chimney sweeps seemed to fade away little by little and their final demise came with the advent of professional cleaners who were equipped with modern vacuum cleaning apparatus.

SEASONS

The type of work which had to be done on the land and in and around each house did not vary much from farm to farm nor from parish to parish. In the Springtime each farmer had to decide on which fields he wished to till for the various crops; the ones to keep for meadow grass and those for pasture. When the ploughing was complete the farmyard manure was carted to the fields and spread uniformly on the ridges and drills where potatoes and root crop seeds were sown. Within a short time the seeds produced new life and fresh shoots appeared above the soil. Nature did the rest but it needed a little help. Turnips and similar crops had to be thinned and weeds had to be pulled from around the new growths of root crops in order to give the latter a better opportunity to survive and thrive. Because much of the soil was disturbed during the weeding operation it was necessary to remould drills and ridges.

The next task was cutting and spreading the turf. Once again nature needed a little help from the farmer and his family to save it. The turf was first cut with a slean and then spread out to dry – sod by sod. Next it was "footed". Footing turf was a simple but back breaking operation. The sods were put standing against one another in small heaps touching at the top only and were a few inches apart at the bottom. Having been placed standing thus the wind got through them and with even the minimum of sunshine they dried out. The final product was then drawn by horse and cart to the farmyard and stacked in a rick if there was no turf shed.

As Summer arrived the first crop in the fields to reach maturity was the meadow grass. (From habitual usage of the description "cutting the meadow" the word "grass" was eventually omitted when referring to the actual crop). This was cut down mainly with scythes in the months of June and July. With favourable weather it was turned and saved into hay within a few days, and in due course it was taken to the haggard and made into a rick. Very few small farmers had haysheds until after the war years.

The harvesting of grain crops took place in early Autumn after which it was the turn of potatoes, turnips and mangolds. Beet was the only crop harvested in Winter and very few people in Garryedmond sowed it. It was messy work and very laborious as each vegetable had to be pulled by hand, then cleaned of clay and finally crowned, that is the top leaves cut off. It was afterwards placed in large heaps on the roadside margins where it was later filled with forks into lorries and transported to Tuam sugar factory.

Activity on the land was at its quietest in Winter but this was the busiest time in and around the house. During Summer and Autumn all the farm animals remained out on the pastures day and night but, with the exception of sheep, they were housed during the Winter. As a result they had to be fed with hay, while cows and young calves were also given drinks and occasionally meal or nuts. All were supplied with beds of straw nightly and the stables or byres were cleaned each morning. Every evening a supply of water from the well had to be in store for household use and also a large container of turf to keep huge fires going until bedtime which was usually around midnight.

Cows were milked by hand each morning and evening throughout the year. Some of the milk was fed to calves and pigs, some was used for household consumption and the remainder was placed in either large brown crocks or white enamel basins. Milk went thick and slightly sour within a few days and the cream was skimmed from it, put into the churn and converted into butter.

Animals knew either by instinct or from repetition the time to return to be housed each night and the same applied to hens, ducks and geese. When the fowl went inside their respective abodes the doors were closed to ensure that no marauding fox entered during the night. The farmer's wife performed a task with ducks during the laying season. After following them into their habitat, she "tried" each of them to check on how many had eggs almost ready to lay. The operation consisted of placing the palm of her hand flat under their tails and she would feel the egg if one was there. If, for example, she had fifteen ducks and twelve had tested positively when "tried," there should be twelve eggs in the nests on the floor the next morning. If there were less than that number all the birds were kept indoors until the last egg was laid. Had this precaution not been taken, the eggs would be laid somewhere in the pastures where no doubt they would be spotted and quickly devoured by hawks or magpies.

THATCHING

Today it is almost impossible to find a person capable of thatching a roof whereas in the thirties and forties practically every man in a farming community could perform the task. Rye straw was preferable for thatching but oaten was acceptable, and having been threshed, it was drawn, which meant that it was flattened out and all creases removed. Thin sally (willow) rods were already cut to lengths of about three feet and after both ends were pointed they were called scollops. The sally, being pliable, bent easily and when the thatcher placed sections of drawn straw tightly together on the roof to a depth of about six inches he bent approximately nine inches of each end of a scollop to a right angle and then pressed it down over the straw to keep it in position. He continued thus until the whole roof was covered.

Depending on the weather encountered, the skill of the thatcher and the quality of the straw, the duration of the roof varied from two to four years. Some people thatched each side of their houses in alternate years and occasionally after a period of excessively wet weather it was necessary to do a patching job, chiefly around the chimney, if there was raindown.

When a roof was newly thatched, especially when oaten straw was used, and the walls were then given a fresh coat of whitewash the contrasting white and golden colours made an attractive sight. The few thatched houses that remain in the country are constantly being photographed by foreign and native tourists alike and they appear in picture postcards around the world.

The picturesque village of Kilmore Quay in Co. Wexford is unique in so far as it has held on to the old tradition of thatched houses, and it draws thousands of visitors annually who come to view the quaint structures that have practically disappeared from the rest of the country. Even when thatch was the familiar roof in rural Ireland, Kilmore Quay was uncommon because many of its houses, which are unchanged today and are still inhabited, were two storeys high. This model was almost totally nonexistent in the west of Ireland.

As time goes by and the memory of thatch fades further into the past, the attraction of Kilmore Quay will become even more alluring. Long may it continue to hold on to its tradition.

THE IMPORTANCE OF GOOD HEALTH

Farmers and their wives did not take holidays until they were advanced in years and had members of their families ready to take the responsibility of running the farm. The Canary Islands, or Bahamas or such exotic resorts were far from their minds. They were more than happy to spend a week in Lecanvey, Salthill or Enniscrone when the highlights of the vacations were their indulgence in seaweed baths which were believed to be health giving. Occasionally a couple went to Lisdoonvarna if either suffered from rheumatism. Many were convinced, possibly with some justification, that if they partook of a sulphur bath each day and drank water from the local iron and magnesia spas their old joints would became limber again.

Except to attend funerals or visit a relative or friend who was ill, young able bodied country folk did not take time off from work unless they became temporarily ill themselves, and the sickness would be severe before they would spend a day in bed. Sending for a doctor was the last straw and this course was decided upon only after much family consultation and after all known quack remedies had failed. They would not want the neighbours to know that there was any kind of sickness in the house. This attitude may have been allied to some degree with the investigation into pedigree, respectability, family connections and good health when any member of a family was seeking a spouse or when a match was introduced. At any rate the doctor was called only when it was deemed absolutely necessary.

It was also important that the health history of animals was known to be good. Diseases, colloquially known as "blackleg," "hoose" and "red water" were believed to be peculiar to particular farms so it would have an adverse effect on sales when animals from such farms were presented at a fair. By chance I actually witnessed the secret burial of a dead two years old bullock at two o'clock one morning by a farmer and his son. It was their hope that by bringing the carcass to their nearby bog under cover of darkness they could conceal the loss. The death of an animal was bad enough but for the neighbours to become aware of such an occurrence was almost unbearable.

CONVERSATION

People looked forward to the relaxation of the long Winter nights. As dusk approached the oil lamp was taken down, the globe or chimney was cleaned, the bowl was filled with paraffin oil and the wick set alight. Even if women worked at sewing or darning and men made baskets or "skibs" from sally rods or put homemade handles on broken rakes and hayforks there was no rush or anxiety to have work complete and they stopped whenever they felt so inclined. There were interruptions for tea and whenever a visitor entered. Visitors were always welcome in every house. There were no formal invitations and callers did not feel obliged to knock on the door. They just lifted the latch and walked in.

The radio was turned on for the news and usually switched off immediately afterwards. The reason for turning it off was twofold. In these days before rural electrification the radio was operated by batteries – one dry and one wet. The life of the dry one expired after a couple of months in use and it had to be replaced by a new one. The other lasted for about two years but it had to be recharged every few weeks in a radio store or garage or such other place as had charging apparatus. Batteries were expensive and conveying the wet one on the carrier of a bicycle when bringing it to be recharged was a difficult chore. Naturally using the radio as little as possible ensured that the batteries lasted longer.

However the second and main reason was the desire to get back to conversation whether or not there were visitors. Guests would not be insulted by leaving a radio rumbling during their visit, unless there was a special programme on in which everybody present was interested.

NEWS OF THE KIRKINTILLOCK TRAGEDY

Much conversation centred around prices for livestock, the weather and the crops but everything that happened in the locality was of interest. If a neighbour emigrated, joined the gardaí, got a job in a shop or garage in the town, or if a baby was born or a match made it was all deserving of discussion. Sometimes ghost stories were told, as were tales of the penal times or historic events like the night of the big wind. Current events were analysed and one of my most abiding memories is of discussions night after night in 1937 of the Kirkintilloch Disaster when ten young Irish potato workers were burned to death in a bothy in Scotland. Their bodies were taken home for burial to their native Achill and passed through Garryedmond by train on the way. They were buried in Kildownet cemetery in one common grave. The tragedy made world headlines at the time and the inhuman conditions under which so many of our emigrants worked and lived were highlighted.

On every one of the many occasions we holidayed in Achill I made a point of visiting their single mass grave which lies almost in the shadow of the Castle of Gráinne Uaile. On my first ever trip to Scotland I made a pilgrim journey to Kirkintilloch. The local library staff, who were most courteous and helpful, allowed me to go through files of local Scottish newspapers which were in circulation during the time of that traumatic event. After some hours of perusal I was provided with photocopies of the reports and hereunder is quoted the last verse of a poem by an unnamed author taken from these files.

"Their cruel deaths shall be recalled
Through years are to come
Those poor ill-fated Irish lads
Far from their native home.
The 'Bothy Fire' shall be retold
'Midst sorrow still profound
May they rest in peace that sleep today
In lonely Achill Sound."

CUSTOMS AND SUPERSTITIONS

It was sometimes difficult to differentiate between old customs and superstitions but some were clear enough. Many customs revolved around death. For instance when a person died all clocks in that house were stopped at the exact time of expiration. The reason was because most callers who came to pay their respects inquired about the time of death so the stopped clock gave the answer.

In the graveyards, lay people were buried facing the east as that is the direction from which the Lord is expected to come on the Last Day. The clergy were excepted because they will come along with Him to introduce us. In some places this custom still abides and where priests are buried in family graves they are often laid in the opposite direction to the other occupants.

What was definitely superstitious was the sowing of a type of weed high on the gables of old houses called "Buachaill an Tigh" which in English means "the boy of the house." It was believed to be a protection against the wiles of the fairies. It did not grow prolifically and apparently needed very little moisture. Although seldom trimmed, it's diameter was usually no more than about ten inches.

Many otherwise sensible people would not interfere with a lone bush, especially a whitethorn, fearing bad luck if they did so. It was quite common to see one growing in the centre of a field, and although most inconvenient, the farmer would plough around it when preparing to sow his crops. Some feared that interference might upset the fairies who inhabited the immediate vicinity, while others who did not believe in these little elves still thought it was better to take no chances.

It was believed by some that it would bring bad luck if an extension was built on to a dwelling house in a particular direction. Depending on which part of the country one lived that direction could be north, south, east or west. If somebody defied the bad luck and if a member of that household died, had a bad accident or suffered any other misfortune even twenty years later there was sure to be a whisper that it happened because of the building. A neighbour could have far worse misfortune but it would go unnoticed.

Some men feared that they would have bad luck for that day if the first person they met in the morning was a red-haired woman. Men travelling to fairs or going on other journeys were known to have returned immediately to their homes following such encounters. They did not seem to realise that bad luck could strike at home also.

Fear of curses was very real among superstitious people and a threat of a widow's curse struck special terror into their hearts.

The number thirteen was deemed by some to be unlucky. That belief has not yet died out completely for it is quite common to see the thirteenth house in a terrace or in an estate numbered "12a". Many hotels and guesthouses skip "thirteen" when numbering their bedrooms. There is an old theory that the superstitions arose from reference to Jesus and the twelve apostles. Judas was the thirteenth. Strangely in some continental countries thirteen is regarded as a lucky number. Perhaps they put the apostles first.

A custom which still exists is for callers to leave a house through the same door as they entered. It was once reckoned that if they went out through a different door they might bring the good luck of the house with them. Scarcely anybody believes that now but visitors are still cautious in case the inhabitants have lingering doubts and they would not wish to hurt their feelings.

Friday was the lucky day to move into a new house or to take up a new job. However it was an unlucky day for a wedding. June was a lucky month for getting married while the opposite applied to May. There was an old saying concerning getting married in May "The month of May, you'll rue the day." A girl from Garryedmond got married on a Friday in May in the early twenties despite her family and neighbours advising her to choose a different day and month. After a number of years the couple parted which was most unusual in those days. Many local people were convinced that the marriage failure was due to the unlucky day and month deliberately selected by them.

When I was a very young boy a casual labourer came to us every Winter and he stayed with us for three or four weeks before moving on to other local farmers for similar periods. Each Spring he went to England to work as a migratory labourer and he remained there until Autumn. There was always welcome for him because although there was little for him to do at that time of the year he worked for his keep only, but was given a present of a few pounds on his departure. On awakening one morning he noted that his watch had stopped. As there was no apparent reason for the stoppage he accused my mother of "putting a bad eye on it." This was supposed to be some kind of a curse. Genuinely believing that there could be no other explanation he became very agitated and, packing his case, he went away never to return to us.

UNHURRIED COUNTRY LIFE

Although the mood of rural Ireland was unhurried and carefree there was seldom an idle moment. With a spade and a "drag" the farmer did whatever draining was necessary and he ensured that all fences were kept in order. Thrift was very important, especially during the war years so he mended shoes and replaced soles and heels as required. He made gates from slender tree branches, always using the minimum amount of nails, some of which were retrieved from broken doors. Neighbouring men cut or clipped each other's hair while visiting, and most of them never saw the inside of a barber's shop.

During my youth I never heard the word "boredom" used, although all forms of entertainment and of travel were by modern standards very limited. There was no luxury in a country house other than the big glowing fire on the open hearth. That might be the only form of physical heating but there was also warmth within the hearts of the country folk. They had time for discussion and time for each other when the pace of life was slower and when, except for the passing trains, only natural sounds broke the stillness. The horse neighing, the donkey braying and the sheep bleating combined blissfully with the song of the thrush from the whitethorn and the cry of the curlew from over the meadows. Now it is the jets flying overhead, tractors rumbling on every farm, television switched on throughout the day, transistor radios blaring and pollution on every side. That, of course is progress and as such it must be welcomed, but it still seems lamentable that most people are now hurrying so much that they do not see nor appreciate the beauty of nature and its dumb creatures which are getting more rare in variety as well as in number with each passing year. In the not too distant future we are likely to hear the bray of a donkey as seldom as we now hear the call of the near extinct corncrake.

Country life, despite all these changes will always have advantages for young people growing up close to nature where they can witness at first hand the mating of animals and birds, see new life entering the world and enjoy the natural environment removed from the glass and concrete jungle of modern urbanisation.

The experience gives a better understanding of nature and a respect for all life and for the God-given wonders of reproduction, and also an appreciation of the magic of falling rain and running streams as well as the changing seasons that never let us down.

John and Mary Costello, the author's grandparents

The author's parents, Willie and Rose with their eldest child John, taken c.1918, outside the family home in Garryedmond

Right to left: The author aged seven, with his brothers John and Séamus and the family dog "Sergeant"

Cogavins of Ballinasloe taken in 1947

The author mowing the meadow in the Acre field in 1953

The author attending to his beehives in Garryedmond c.1958

The Committee who compiled the history of the Mayo Association,Galway "Seventeen Years a-Growing"at the launch of the book in 1988.
Back left to right: **Jimmy Woolley (Claremorris); KevinDuffy (Kiltimagh); Bernard O'Hara (Swinford); Sean McManamon (Claremorris) Andy Dunleavy (Crossmolina).** *Front:* **Bernadette Browne (Swinford); Willie Costello (Claremorris); Mary Hughes (Westport).**

The author and his wife, Bernadette, on their wedding day, 11 August 1958

Members of Mayo Co. Council taken in 1966, left to right:
Michael Fadian; Joe McManamon; Jimmy Grennan; Tommy O'Hara; Tom Durkin; Tom Bourke; Martin J. McGrath; John O'Donnell (Co. Sec.); Patrick Quinn; Dalgan Lyons; P. J. Campbell; Willie Costello, the author; Joe Lenehan; Jack Garret; Tommy Thornton; Martin Finn; Owen Hughes; Sean T. Ruane; Douglas Kelly; Joe Blowick and Sonny Holster.
(photo courtesy of "Connaught Telegraph")

16

Memorable Individuals

PAT LALLY

Pat Lally lived very close to us so my memories of him go back almost to my infancy. Like all those living around us he would be classed as a good neighbour. He never gave offence to anybody but he loved deep discussions especially those pertaining to religion. Every single night with his wife Kate he was host to a full house of visitors, some of them playing "25". Pat did not play cards but he entertained all present with his funny stories and witty comments. When card playing was over and we sat around the fire drinking tea Pat was likely to pose one of his theological kind of questions of which the following is typical. "We will suppose that I wanted to get a Mass said for my intentions and I asked you to oblige me by calling to the priest on my behalf with an offering of one pound which I gave you. You agreed, and you told me later that you had complied with my request. But instead of calling on the priest you kept the pound yourself. Now would I get the benefit of the Mass?"

If you answered that he probably would, seeing that he gave the stipend and believed that the Mass was offered he would counter "But how could I get the benefit if the Mass was not said?"

On the other hand if you said "No" he would say, "but we have always been told that God is all justice and mercy and surely He wouldn't deprive me of the benefit, seeing that my intention was good and as far as I was concerned I had given the offering to the priest?" Although Pat did not have the answers either he always appeared to get the upper hand in discussions.

A point I heard him make more than once was that the Pope and the clergy were insincere when they impressed on us that we should always have faith and accept the Will of God. "Now" Pat would say "everything that happens is the will of God. If God did not will it, He would not allow it to happen. But if the Pope gets sick he immediately sends for his doctor. If he had the faith that he preaches he would not send for the doctor. He would just pray and wait to see what was the Will of God."

Pat was a man of common sense and of deep faith himself. He did not believe that the Pope was hypocritical but he loved to generate discussions of this type which he knew everybody enjoyed.

My brother Séamus and Pat were once discussing the then recent death of a local elderly lady who had lived a life of great piety, bereft of any kind of extravagance and who was generous and charitable in the extreme. Séamus said "If she has not got to Heaven there is not much hope for the rest of us."

"That is true," agreed Pat.

As an afterthought he added "On the other hand if we DO get to Heaven isn't she nicely codded?"

Pat lived in a comfortable bungalow but like most other people of his time he was born in a thatched house which remained his home until long after he got married. He told many exaggerated stories of the "rain-down" which took place in it after periods of wet weather. "Rain-down" was a term used for the seepage of rain through thatched roofs which left ugly streaks, yellowed by smoke, on the walls and which indeed was not unusual. During his youth he slept in the "hag" bed as did his younger brother John who later emigrated to America. On his return from visiting one very wet night he entered as quietly as possible because his mother and the other members of her family were asleep. Amidst the silence there was an unusual noise coming from the "hag" where John was in bed and it sounded like a clock ticking loudly. When he pushed aside the curtain to investigate, John handed out to him a large basin full with water saying "Hand me in the bath to hold the rain water – this container is full." The tick-tock noise came from the rain dropping with a regular beat into the basin.

There was probably an element of truth in the story but as the old saying goes, "he didn't take anything off it."

NED BYRNE

Ned Byrne was a native of Bekan from where in his very early years he emigrated to America and he returned to Ireland in the mid thirties. While in the States he studied at night schools securing diplomas so on his return to the homeland he was a learned, self-educated man.

His interest in literature was profound and unusual for a man who, apart from his comparitively short time in America, spent his whole life at farming. He had a library of rare books and was only too pleased to lend them to anybody who was interested in them. The writings of Thomas Moore had a special appeal for him and while capable of reciting by heart many of his poems he always looked beyond the words to imbibe their true meaning. He also had many proverbs which he loved to quote if an appropriate occasion presented itself. Examples were "Eagles' eggs, they still make eagles, and wherever they are hatched they are eagles still," and "Common sense is not so common."

When he arrived on the farm in Caraun, Ned was eyed by the neighbours with a certain amount of curiosity. He purchased the most modern machinery available at that time, including a horse-drawn hay rake-cum-gatherer and a tedder or hay shaker. They were the first implements of their type ever to appear in our district. Of course he also had a mowing machine, but while most farmers mowed meadows with scythes there were a few machines about.

Progressive in his farming methods, he was the first to make hay cocks without one person going up on each cock and tramping it. In that way six or seven could be made within the time that one would be made using the traditional method. The neighbours said that the hay would rot. There was no scientific basis for the prediction but it was such a change from the practice of generations that they thought it had to be wrong. Sure he was a Yank and would know nothing about farming would sum up their attitude. However when the time came to bring the hay into the haggard or hayshed it was at least as good as that which the neighbour had tramped. It might have been even better. Despite this evidence it was quite a few years before every farmer in the locality was cocking hay in the new, quicker and less laborious way.

Over the years he was a constant visitor to our house, regaling us with stories of his experiences abroad and generously sharing his vast knowledge of local history. When he died in 1987 at the age of eighty-three I felt the same sense of loss as I would for a very close relative.

PAT COMER

Pat Comer was a brother of Mike to whom I have referred earlier but he possessed a totally different kind of personality. While Mike was quiet and serious Pat was flamboyant and highly entertaining. He usually remained at home at night with his sister Mary and a number of visitors who listened eagerly to the tall stories he told of his escapades and adventures of many years earlier. None of the three Comers married.

Pat could be described as one of the two unqualified local veterinary surgeons in our community. Whenever there was a problem in the district with sheep yeaning, mares foaling or cows calving, Pat was called. He was obviously gifted in this pursuit as was proven by his success. Maybe he was just lucky but anyway it was seldom a real veterinary surgeon had to be called to any farm in our area, in the days before testing and tagging were introduced.

JOHN RUANE

Skilled in a different branch of veterinary science was another neighbour named John Ruane. His importance in the neighbourhood was readily acknowledged but when early Summer approached, we, as children, hated him. For he was the man who performed operations to neuter the male lambs and calves. He also cut off the lambs' tails – a surgery regarded as essential for reasons of hygiene.

His standards of work would not be accepted today. There was no sterilisation other than a squirt of Jeyes Fluid or diluted Lysol and his only surgical implement or scalpel was a sharp penknife. There was no anaesthetic so the poor animals were tied or held down during the operation while they roared in pain. Was it any wonder that we did not exactly love him? But he was held in high regard by our parents and we too soon forgot the episodes of cruelty when the animals recovered. When we grew up we realised that these were necessary evils on a farm and it was marvellous to have an obliging neighbour so close at hand. Needless to say there was never a question of any payment in money or in kind for any of his services and the same applied to Pat Comer.

In my childhood days John Ruane lived next door to us with his brother Austin and their aging parents. To describe them as owners of a stud farm would be an exaggeration, but for many decades they kept two bulls and a stallion for hire. These were huge animals and to a child they looked even bigger. Because bulls were known to be dangerous and liable to attack and kill, we gave them a wide berth. While still a yearling calf, the bull's nose was penetrated with a red hot iron rod and a ring inserted in it. When the animal matured and was about to become dangerous a heavy chain was hung from the ring. He was thereby prevented from running fast because of the weight of the chain and he was also likely to stand on it when it would trip him and hurt. Fortunately none of the bulls owned by the Ruanes ever attacked or injured anybody.

TOM FOY

Tom Foy who died in 1942 at the age of thirty three was, in his day, the most prominent man in Garryedmond. I always felt that he was about a quarter of a century ahead of his time and now on reflection I am convinced that double that time would be nearer the mark.

His father died leaving a wife and five children when Tom, who was the eldest, was still a child. These were the days prior to Widows Pensions, Childrens' Allowances, or any other kind of State help. When he left Koilmore national school he was interested in becoming a carpenter but as he was required at home to work on the land his mother could not afford to let him go to serve his apprenticeship.

He did not lose interest however, and from calling into workshops in the town whenever feasible and watching carpenters at work and having discussions with them he learned a little about the trade. One Winter while still a teenager he purchased a few tools and some timber and set about making a horse cart which by the following spring he had complete. With the exception of the wheels and fittings which he had to purchase, it was entirely his own workmanship.

About that time his friend and neighbour, Jim Cunnane from Caraun who was a carpenter procured a large premises in The Square, Claremorris where he opened a hardware shop and in the yard he established a builders' providers business. He went into building contracting in a big way, employing many men. Among them was Tom Foy, who commenced at the base digging foundations, mixing concrete and changing casings. The cavity block was still in the future, as was the raft or floating foundation. Within a short time he was promoted to the position of foreman overseeing the work of a large number of employees.

Having gained knowledge of all aspects of building he branched out on his own and became an instant success. He purchased a new lorry on the doors of which were painted in large letters "T. Foy, Builder and Contractor, Garryedmond, Claremorris." The same words on the large hoardings on his various sites were a source of pride to his neighbours who were thrilled to see the success of the energetic young entrepreneur.

He also purchased a luxurious motor car at a time when any kind of a car was indeed a luxury. Apart from the numerous houses which he built throughout South Mayo the most enduring monuments to his craft and to his memory are in Claremorris town where stand the Central Cinema, now closed, and The Savoy Ballroom of which he was joint owner.

Standing about six feet three inches, with blue eyes and a fine crop of wavy fair hair, Tom certainly "cut a great dash," and was a great favourite among young ladies. He was the first person I ever saw in a dress suit and in all probability his was the first one ever purchased by a Garryedmond man. At that time the coat was called a swallow tail, and was often facetiously referred to as a claw hammer. Twenty years later the tuxedo had almost completely replaced the swallow tail at all dress functions.

Perhaps Tom Foy never accumulated much material wealth but he earned big money which he was not afraid to spend. He was a familiar figure at hunt balls in various parts of the country and on his many visits to the capital he always stayed in the Gresham Hotel.

Despite all the foregoing he was totally unpretentious at heart and, although enjoying living it up, he was equally happy strolling in to the local houses on a Sunday afternoon, having a chat and drinking a cup of tea. Sadly, death claimed him when he was only entering the prime of life and had fate been different we can only speculate on what might have been.

THE PRENDERGASTS

There were regular coursing meetings held in Dillon's field in Claremorris during the thirties. This is a very emotional subject at present which raises the hackles in some quarters whenever it is mentioned. But in the thirties and forties it was just another sport. So quite a few people in the parish had thoroughbred greyhounds but the only Garryedmond owner to hit the high spots in my time was Maggie Prendergast.

With other members of her family she had a long history of involvement with the industry cum sport. Her most successful dog was purchased as a pup from James Murphy the local school teacher and she named him "Londuff".

He won several prizes, and with her brother, Bally, Maggie travelled to coursing meetings far and wide. The many successes of Londuff gave the local people an added interest in coursing as they followed his fortunes.

Maggie had three other brothers John, David and Michael who for some reason was known as "Gawdy." John died from the infamous 1918 flu which raged throughout Europe following the first World War but I have a clear recollection of the other members of the family and of their passion for greyhounds.

FATHER JIMMY GIBBONS

Fr. Jimmy Gibbons was not a native of Claremorris but he left his mark on the parish in a manner which has been equalled by few who were born there. He exerted an influence on the people that surpassed that of any other person of his time. A man of great energy and vision he encouraged the whole populace to believe in themselves and to get up off their knees in the dark period of penury and low morale in the nineteen fifties. Forced emigration was then as rife as at any time since the famine and what was worse, the hope for a brighter future entered the minds of few.

To the forefront in the field of culture and physical development for the youth, he was the mainspring in the upsurge of G.A.A. activity locally, and it was his enthusiasm and enterprise that spurred local followers to purchase the building at Courthouse Road and the football pitch. He did not fear going into debt so long as a spirit of unity and of purpose existed, and he counselled that if people were prepared to work together they could overcome almost any obstacle.

He was the driving force that succeeded in getting "the creamery" for Claremorris. This was a tedious and laborious process. It commenced as a separating station at Courthouse Road after successful negotiation with Gurteen creamery whose management supplied the machinery, the transport and the expertise. Prior to that an extensive canvass of farming support took place over an extensive area. Their financial support was almost as necessary as their guarantee to supply milk. Its success ensured that for the first time the farming community in the district secured what had always been missing, namely, stable monthly cheques. The progress of that enterprise can be seen today in the huge business conducted in the local N.C.F. premises to which it has evolved.

Father Jimmy did all his work without blowing his own trumpet or looking for any credit. The knowledge that his tenure in Claremorris would be short was proof of no personal interests in the projects which he spearheaded. The success of his efforts on behalf of his flock was more than ample reward.

Apart from his work in the material sense he was also a great spiritual counsellor and a friend to anyone in distress. He was a gifted preacher and his sermons are still a source of conversation more than a quarter of a century after his departure from the parish.

Father Jimmy, who was a native of Westport, was for a time afterwards a curate in Mayo Abbey before his appointment as Parish Priest of Menlough. Later, on becoming Parish Priest of Athenry, he was appointed a Canon which position he held at the time of his death in 1982.

THE FLANNERYS OF CLOONTOOA

Mary Ann Flannery was a quiet, inoffensive lady from Cloontooa. She did not marry and she lived with her bachelor brother John in what had once been their small farmhouse. Built into a little hillock and scarcely worthy of being described as a house, in time it became almost submerged in the ground, and the thatched roof was nearly flat. With the exception of the front wall which contained a door and a window the remainder of the building was on the same level as the ground around. It stood near the centre of a field and there was no roadway leading to it.

They sold their little farm long before I was born and when I first got to know them they were both in late middle age. During Mary Ann's lifetime John was seldom seen out of doors. She went to Claremorris on foot once every week – a journey of more than five miles – and was known to collect "outdoor relief." From this money, her groceries were purchased which she carried home in a handbag. They never asked anybody for anything but neither did they ever refuse benevolence from neighbours. Indeed they gratefully accepted food, turf and clothing when it was offered.

Mary Ann was known to pretty well everybody in Claremorris and to all who lived along the five mile road from her home. She was conspicuous because of the peculiarity of her dress. She wore the same multicolour arrayment of clothing when the Summer sun was scorching and when Winter frost was biting. An assortment of at least three jumpers or cardigans each showing untidily but clearly were to be seen. One might be bright yellow, another deep red and the third green or blue. Similarly her skirts varied in colour, with the outer one ten or fifteen inches shorter than the ones beneath.

She was ever quiet and dignified. Never the first one to speak, but when addressed her response was polite and she was quite capable of holding an informed conversation.

After her death John was forced to make the weekly journey to the town. He too was courteous and dignified. He was conservative in dress, usually wearing a dark suit and hat, and in cold weather a long black overcoat. I often met him and it was a pleasure to have discussions with him. He had no radio, but he read newspapers and was very enlightened in current affairs. But far more entertaining and informative were his reminiscences of his early days. His stories and recollections of the Boer War, the sinking of The Titanic, the Indian Mutiny and the fate of local members of the Connacht Rangers and other big events of those far off days were spellbinding.

It is many years since the Flannerys passed on. They had no close relatives but were distant cousins of a well known politician. I think it is fitting to include them among the memorable people whom I knew. They owned no property, scarcely ever travelled outside the parish, did not visit in neighbouring houses and nobody entered their own. They never did anything exciting nor achieve anything as far as human eyes could see but they had attributes of which few can boast. They were never known to gossip nor to utter an unkind word. They injured nobody by word or deed and they interfered with nobody.

Perhaps they achieved more than any of us.

MICHAEL RONAYNE

Michael Ronayne was a native of Irishtown but spent his working life in Claremorris where he used his inventive and entrepreneurial skills to good effect. He started business making egg boxes in a small workshop in Church Street and while there invented the cubicle egg box which saved eggs from breaking during rough handling of the containers.

About 1930 he founded Claremorris Brush Company and he built a factory on the site where the cattle mart now operates. For close on thirty years he gave good employment to local young men and women and when the factory was at its peak there were one hundred and fifty people on the payroll. A wide assortment of brushes was produced including bottle brushes and polish brushes but he concentrated on manufacturing whitewash, distemper and paint brushes, twigs, domestic sweeping brushes and bass brooms which were more commonly known as yard brushes.

While it was described as a brush factory a variety of other items were also made at the new plant. They included kitchen chairs, bar stools, and spokes, stocks and felloes for cart wheels, but their best known product apart from brushes was their aptly named "Favourite" washboard which outsold those of all competitors at that time.

Manufacturing was not the only activity within the factory walls. Michael was a founder member and patron of Claremorris Boxing Club and at great inconvenience to his employees and to himself he allowed a portion of the building to be used free of charge as a training arena. Many boxing tournaments took place there when contenders fought for provincial and national titles. Although boxing never appealed to me I went to see some tournaments and training sessions there.

The factory closed down during the recession in 1957. Markets had deteriorated, there were no Government grants available for refurbishment or replacement of machinery and the E.E.C. gravy train had not yet arrived. Banks were not only unhelpful but very cruel. Like every closure it was a great loss to all concerned, and among those who lost their full-time employment in the factory were Michael's sons, Sean and J. J. In later times J. J. set up a smaller operation at Convent Road, making brushes only, and it is still going well.

Michael Ronayne's interests went far beyond the activities of the factory. He was one of the pioneers of the idea of purchasing land on which to build private houses. He transformed the Brookhill road, and the houses he erected there are a monument to his forward thinking. They enhance the area to this day and help to blend the very old buildings in the district with the ultra modern.

He also had a great interest in horses and was owner of a number of show jumpers. They were ridden by his sons J.J., Philip and Jarlath.

Incidentally Jarlath is now Vice Chancellor of the University of Melbourne and he recently presided at the conferring of an honorary doctorate on former Taoiseach Albert Reynolds.

During the years of World War Two when private motor cars were taken off the roads, the pony and trap came back into fashion as a necessary form of transport. This renaissance encouraged people to build ornate horse-drawn carriages, and at most sports meetings and agricultural shows there were driving competitions with prizes for those best turned out. Michael had his own carriage built and was awarded many prizes at various Connacht venues.

Throughout his life Michael Ronayne was an ardent nationalist and he took great pride in the part his father played in helping Michael Davitt to found the Land League. There is a story told that on an occasion when trying to negotiate a loan he was invited to the office of a bank manager who did not share his republican views. It was a few days before the twelfth of July, and on entering he saw hanging over the chair positioned for clients an Orangeman's sash which the manager intended to wear when marching in Belfast later in the week. Before sitting down, Michael reached for the sash and placed it aside stating that he could not discuss business with such an emblem hanging over him. Needless to say he did not get the loan and local people believe that the harsh treatment subsequently meted out to him by the same bank manager when his factory was in financial difficulty had its basis in the incident concerning the Orange sash.

Michael Ronayne, who died in 1958, was a very progressive individual who in his day put much effort into improving the economic, social and cultural life of Claremorris. He should not be forgotten.

EAMONN HUGHES

I was only sixteen years old when Eamonn Hughes asked me to accept a role in a play he had written and was about to put on the stage. He was going to give it the title *White Carnations*. Being an apprentice at the time meant that getting time off for rehearsals would be uncertain, and I definitely would not be afforded the necessary concessions to go to the various venues where he proposed to stage it. So with the greatest regret I turned down the offer.

White Carnations, which he produced and in which he acted, went on to become a great success and it gave its name to the dramatic group founded by him to stage it. He continued to write other plays which were staged by the Carnation Players and by several other amateur dramatic societies in Ireland and abroad. Among the best known were *Keane Wasn't Able, The Old Bucket, Little Tom's Romance* and *The Chestnut.* He won a number of prestigious awards for acting and producing. From his pen also came songs including *By a Fireside in Mayo* and *There's a Peaceful Spot in Ireland,* which are still sung at gatherings both at home and in faraway places when Irish exiles assemble.

My own friendship with Eamonn, which began when *White Carnations* was receiving its final touches, lasted until his recent death. He failed to introduce me to the stage but he succeeded in launching me into public speaking at after-Mass election meetings on behalf of Dr. George Maguire in 1961. My first public address was at a meeting in Irishtown where I was introduced by Eamonn who was an experienced orator and campaigner and he had told me beforehand what to say and how to say it. More importantly perhaps, he told me what I was not to say. On subsequent Sundays we addressed meetings in Ballyglass, Ballindine and Taugheen and probably the experience whetted my appetite to participate in public life in later years.

His passing deprived Claremorris of a worthy son whose creativity, enterprise and enthusiasm brought joy to thousands and put his native town on the national and international map in a unique way.

CARDINAL D'ALTON

John Francis D'Alton was born in Church Street, Claremorris on October 11th 1882, in a house where the D'Alton Inn Hotel stands today. His parents had a bar and grocery business there. His mother was formerly Mrs. Mary Brennan who was a widow when she married James D'Alton. John Francis was their only child, but Mrs. D'Alton had one child in her previous marriage – a daughter, Mollie Brennan. After James D'Alton's death the mother of the future Cardinal was married for the third time to Terence McElroy. They had no family. While he was a Professor in Maynooth College, Dr. D'Alton donated a pulpit to Claremorris Church in memory of his mother. When moving it during recent renovations to the building its structure was found to be irreparably faulty. Although pulpits are now obsolete the disappearance of this relic from the church was unwelcome, but the marble pillars and slabs have found a place in the new altar.

John D'Alton received his early education in Claremorris at the local Convent of Mercy and later in the boys' national school in Church Street. He subsequently became a student in Blackrock College, Dublin, where he was a classmate of Eamon de Valera with whom a life long friendship developed. In due course he entered Holy Cross College, Clonliffe, where he studied for the priesthood and was ordained in The Irish College, Rome, in 1908.

John D'Alton grew up in Claremorris at the same time as my parents, both of whose families were customers in the shop owned by D'Altons and later by McElroys. He was known to them and to everybody in Claremorris as Jackie D'Alton, and although very quiet and studious he was extremely popular. In Ireland he was probably the outstanding classical scholar not only of his generation but of the twentieth century. Among his achievements were a first class honours degree in Arts from The Royal University in 1904; a doctorate in divinity from The Irish College, Rome, in 1908 and an M.A. degree from The National University of Ireland in 1910. For thirty years he lectured in Maynooth College of which Institution he became President in 1936. He became a Monsignor in 1938, a Bishop in 1942, an Archbishop in 1946 and a Cardinal in 1953.

Following his appointment as Cardinal in the same year as he was conferred with the degree of Doctor of Literature by Queens University, Belfast, the people of his native Claremorris arranged a public reception or welcome home party for him. I was proud to be among the thousands who were there to greet him when he arrived in Lower James Street and alighted from the old Rolls Royce which had earlier been the mode of conveyance of Cardinal McRory. We then marched ahead of him to the parish church where he was greeted by Dean Daly before he inspected a Guard of Honour composed of members of the Local Defence Force. As many as could be accommodated entered the church where he spoke briefly from the pulpit which bore his mother's name. He thanked the people for their reception and having referred to the honour conferred on Ireland through him, he expressed his hopes for the future of our country and for the Church.

On the following day a garden party in Saint Colman's College and its grounds was attended by several hundred people. A civic welcome was read by Martin McGrath, Chairman of Mayo County Council and every single person present was introduced individually to the Cardinal. An abundance of tea and delicacies was freely available to all. It was indeed a day to remember.

Throughout his whole life Jackie D'Alton was a great scholarly, but unassuming, man. He never forgot his native Claremorris where he was a regular visitor at the home of his step niece, Nora Maguire and her husband Doctor George Maguire. Almost every year he holidayed with them in Achill Island.

Tommy Higgins who built the D'Alton Inn Hotel on the site of his birth place, named that establishment after the Cardinal. So did the Western Health Board when naming the new Retirement Home in Convent Road, and during his lifetime the people of the town changed the name of the street where he was born from Church Street to D'Alton Street.

Despite those honours, it can not be denied that in 1982, the centenary year of his birth, more could have been done to mark the occasion. If other towns could have laid claim to his birthplace more would have been made of the situation, as witness for example the honouring of Margaret Burke Sheridan in Castlebar or John McBride in Westport.

John Francis D'Alton, who died in 1963 and was buried in the grounds of Armagh Cathedral, was one of only nine Irish Cardinals ever appointed and the only one born West of the Shannon. He was an international figure who brought fame and credit to his own family, to his native parish, to his county and to his country.

DELIA MURPHY

Delia Murphy, who became known as Ireland's Ballad Queen, was born in Ardroe, Claremorris on 16th February 1902, although many commentators and scribes have claimed that she was born in Mountjennings near Hollymount. Perhaps she should have been born in Mountjennings as this was probably what her parents intended. Her father, John Murphy, was a native of Cloondinnaire a few miles from Claremorris on the Ballyglass road. His niece Hannah still resides there on the old family farm. As a young man he emigrated to the United States and for some years he worked in the Klondike goldmines in Colorado. After his marriage he returned to Ireland with his wife when they purchased Mountjennings house and farm. For some legal reason they were unable to get immediate possession and while awaiting the settling of the transfer of deeds they rented a house in Ardroe near the present abode of Tom and Ann Veldon. It was there that Delia was born. Perhaps fate was unkind to Mountjennings in view of the worldwide fame and acclamation which Delia later achieved, but facts are facts. However, Delia and her parents took up residence in Mountjennings within a short time of her birth.

From there she attended Gortskehi national school – a building which I entered many times myself on business calls in later years. Having completed her secondary education in the Dominican Convent in Eccles Street, Dublin, she entered University College, Galway, from where she graduated with a Bachelor of Commerce degree. It was there she first met her future husband Dr. Thomas J. Kiernan who was lecturing in economics. After entering the Diplomatic Service he was posted to Embassies around the world and wherever he went Delia was at his side. As the wife of a distinguished Ambassador she rubbed shoulders with Popes, royalty and statesmen but she never lost the common touch.

As a child she became interested in Irish folk songs and ballads which she heard sung around the local firesides and also by members of the travelling community who camped in the vicinity of her home. She publicly acknowledged having learned some ballads from a traveller child who accompanied her to Gortskehi school.

This interest remained with her throughout her life and she recorded in her own inimitable style, hundreds of old songs and ballads which without her would definitely have been lost. She also composed songs, and thanks to broadcasters like Donnacha Ó Dúlaing, Aidan O'Hara, Ciarán Mac Mathúna and others her records are played regularly over the air waves. Despite her many concerts in all parts of the country over a very long career I saw her only once in a live performance. Her success as a singer and composer of songs was equalled only by the manner in which she found her way into the hearts of all Irish people.

After her death a committee was formed in Roundfort parish which organised the erection of a memorial to her at Killeens Cross beside her old Mountjennings home. I was privileged to be at the unveiling which was attended by several hundred people including Canon W. Walsh, Donnacha Ó Dúlaing, Aidan O'Hara and my own personal friend of many years, Mrs. Mary McGovern, who played a fundamental part in organising the event. Popular Claremorris man Martin Cunniffe, who regrettably has since passed away, entertained us there with songs which he had sung as a boy when he accompanied Delia on many of her concert tours.

Delia Murphy's sister, Angela, was also an accomplished singer but she did not achieve the eminence of her famous sister. Sadly she died early in life. Another sister was married to Paddy Mellott of Prospect House, Crossboyne and their daughter is married to Greg Warde of The Square, Claremorris.

Delia Murphy lived out her final years in The Strawberry Beds near Lucan and she passed to her reward in 1971 having given a lifetime of devotion to her husband who predeceased her by four years; to her family and to Irish songs and traditions. As the centenary of her birth is almost upon us it should not be too much to hope that the occasion will be marked in a manner worthy of her and of all she has done for our native culture. If an individual memorial is not erected to perpetuate her memory at least a public building, perhaps the library, should be named after her and perhaps the road leading to her birthplace might be renamed Bóthar Uí Mhurchú. She deserves our deepest appreciation and Claremorris and Ireland owe her much.

THE MEMORIES ARE MINE

I have titled this chapter "memorable individuals" but I would stress that the memories are mine alone. The selection of a few does not diminish in any way the importance of countless other people who have lived in Claremorris during my time nor does it take from the contributions of some who distinguished themselves in other times but were not known to me personally.

By a Fireside in Mayo

by

EAMONN P. HUGHES.

If I ever leave old Ireland for a home across the sea
There is one place in this fair land will memories bring to me.
When the twilight's softly stealing o'er the plains of old Mayo
Sure I'll miss my Irish fireside and the people I love so.

By a fireside in Mayo I will always wish to be
With the simple folk I know there and the friends so dear to me.
When each dreary day is over how I long to sit and stare
By a fireside in Mayo I forget all earthly care.

By that fireside in Mayo all my troubles are confessed
In the firelight's cheery glow there is happiness and rest.
Oh, I soon may leave old Erin and my heart is filled with care.
But I'll ne'er forget that fireside and the people I love there.

By that fireside in Mayo I will always wish to be
With the simple folk I know there and the friends so dear to me.
When each dreary day is over how I love to sit and stare
By a fireside in Mayo I forget all earthly care
By a fireside in Mayo I forget all earthly care.

(Courtesy of Eamonn Hughes, Claremorris – son of the composer)

17

Conclusion

THE END OF MY RAMBLE

The ramble which I set out to take has come to an end. For me it has been a most fruitful exercise having brought back memories, some of which had lain dormant for decades. Recalling past events automatically helps one to relive many happy adventures of bygone days spent in the company of family, friends and neighbours but equally it renews the pain of countless poignant experiences. This sadness relates mainly to the loss of dear ones. Some are abiding in far distant lands because of emigration but far, far deeper is the wound inflicted by the passing on of those who have died. There is no family that has not experienced bereavement because eventually the end comes to everybody.

When reminiscing on childhood and adolescence there is a tendency to dwell mainly on happy times and think of them as the good old days. But I acknowledge that when growing up many of us had the ambition to get away from the drudgery of rural life and secure a job in a town or a city, in Ireland if possible, but even abroad if needs be. There would be more money for less labour, regular working hours and a better social life with nights and Sundays free. Some achieved that ambition and many of them became wealthy industrialists or business people, and a few became prominent in professions. Others remained at home because they had to take over the family farm and the care of the old folk. Others still had a deep rooted love of the land and of the rural way of life and they stayed by choice.

THE FAR OFF HILLS

Regardless of the place on the map or the stratum of society in which people find themselves there are always the successful and the less than successful. But even where fortune looks kindly there is an inclination among those who remain to question what they might have achieved had they gone away while most of those who go have a longing for the "ould sod" and a desire to return to it. This would seem to confirm the contention of St. Augustine that while we are on this earth regardless of what we achieve there will always be some yearning in the human heart. I am here reminded of a poem we learned in Koilmore school, the author of which is unknown to me, and it would appear to summarise much of the foregoing, implying as it does that the far off hills are not always green.

"The boy in the country labours on
And bears in his breast from dawn to dawn
The eager hope that he yet will be
A man in the city rich and free.

The man in the city plods his way
Worn out by the toil from day to day
And he sighs that he no more can be
A boy in the country glad and free."

A friend of mine from Mayo who is now living in Galway told me recently that some years ago he visited a former school mate who had entered the psychiatric ward of a hospital for treatment. Over the years this patient had become a very wealthy business man and property owner. Due to the strain which sometimes accompanies such success he suffered a temporary nervous breakdown. The patient said to him "Oh! what would I give to be back again turning out turf with an ass and baskets? When doing that I had only stirabout for my breakfast but I was free from stress."

There is much more to entice young people to remain on the land today than there was half a century ago. There is a good standard of living, a tractor on every farm with machinery and electric components to do the slogging that had to be done by hand only a few decades ago. Every home has the same modern comforts as are to be found in those of any city or country in the world. With acceptable roads almost everywhere and comfortable cars to drive on them, whatever entertainment is in the towns is only a few minutes drive away. And, with an international airport down the road, most places in the world are but a few hours away. To the aforementioned may be added that the rural air is still relatively clean and the crime wave, which is so common in urban areas, has remained at bay to a great extent.

NO REGRETS

As was the case with many of my contemporaries it was necessary for me to leave my native parish in order to make a living. But Garryedmond continues to lure me back. Perhaps it is nostalgia for a way of life that will not be seen again, when happiness reigned in the midst of paucity. Scarce were the wordly goods, but however little their possessions they were dispensable when a neighbour's need was deemed to be greater. When the cows went dry, milk was supplied by a neighbour and when circumstances changed the recipient did likewise and supplied another. Work, which depended mainly on good weather for successful harvesting, was instantly dropped at a signal that a neighbour's animal was in distress and help was rendered without concern for the possible loss of their own crops.

But we now live in a world where it is necessary to be pragmatic if we are to survive, so I have no regrets. There is an obligation on all of us to do what seems to be in the best interests of those for whom we have responsibility, and to take advantage of each opportunity that comes our way, for it may knock only once. On the positive side also, I have made countless friends in every part of the country as my work brought me to the four provinces.

My book is an attempt to pass on to posterity memories of an era that was different. While it had boundless disadvantages, and a return to such primitiveness would be unendurable, I am still glad that my birthplace was Garryedmond and that I was there in a time of simplicity and ease when stress and anxiety were virtually unknown. While fate destined that most of my life should be lived elsewhere my spirit remained there.

The Author

Willie Costello was born on a small farm in Garryedmond near Claremorris on 22nd November, 1926. The youngest of three brothers, he went directly from school to serve his apprenticeship in Warde's Hardware, Claremorris, at fifteen years of age. Later he worked in shops in Ballyhaunis and Ballinasloe.

While in hospital recuperating from a protracted illness in the early fifties, he commenced writing and had articles accepted for publication by The Blarney Annual, St. Anthony Annals, and a trade union periodical An Saothraidh Riartha. He continued to write in the last-named for many years.

After returning from hospital to Garryedmond in 1953 he purchased an Adana hand-printing machine and learned how to use it from manuals. Although successful in mastering the skills, he could not make a living on the returns, so he took up a part-time position as night telephone attendant in Claremorris post office, which he held for a period of six years. In conjunction with the post office job he took an agency with a life assurance company and stayed in that business for the remainder of his working life.

In 1963 following the death of Claremorris Co. Councillor John Gilligan, a Fianna Fáil convention selected him as a replacement, and he was co-opted to Mayo Co. Council. He was elected to The Vocational Education Committee, The County Committee of Agriculture, The Mental Health Committee, and to The Western Health Institutions Board. In 1967 he successfully contested the Co. Council election but a year later he was promoted by the assurance company and transferred to Cork, necessitating his resignation from public life. Further promotions followed, to Wexford in 1970 and to Galway in 1977, where he has since lived. Following early retirement he founded a brokerage business, which in its first full year won the prestigious Irish Life Top Brokers Award.

In 1988 he was appointed Ministerial Representative on The Western Health Board; in 1992 he was appointed to The National Social Services Board by the Minister for Health and in 1995 he was elected a director of Age Action (Ireland) Ltd. and re-elected in 1996. He is actively involved in Mayo Association, Galway; in the charitable organisations Slánú and Gorta, and in the cultural and educational groups, Griffon Creative Writers, and Third Age University. His return to writing was an attempt to counteract loneliness following the death of his wife, formerly Bernadette Connally from Castlerea.

He is already working on a second book about his experiences in the insurance world. Stories of bizarre episodes he witnessed and odd, even freakish characters he encountered within the industry will be most revealing.

Index

G

H

I

J

K

L